Disney Connections & Collections

VOLUME TWO:
TV MOVIES AND ANTHOLOGIES

James R. Mason, Ph.D

Theme Park Press
The Happiest Books on Earth
www.ThemeParkPress.com

© 2019 James R. Mason, Ph.D

No part of this publication may be reproduced, distributed, or transmitted in any form or by any means, including photocopying, recording, or other electronic or mechanical methods, without the prior written permission of the publisher, except for brief quotations embodied in critical reviews and certain other non-commercial uses permitted by copyright law.

Although every precaution has been taken to verify the accuracy of the information contained herein, no responsibility is assumed for any errors or omissions, and no liability is assumed for damages that may result from the use of this information.

Theme Park Press is not associated with the Walt Disney Company.

The views expressed in this book are those of the author and do not necessarily reflect the views of Theme Park Press.

Theme Park Press publishes its books in a variety of print and electronic formats. Some content that appears in one format may not appear in another.

Editor: Bob McLain

Layout: Artisanal Text

ISBN 978-1-68390-218-8

Printed in the United States of America

Theme Park Press | www.ThemeParkPress.com

Address queries to bob@themeparkpress.com

To

Ross & Matt

Thanks for your continued support, and for being my first 'customer' of Vol 1!

You're in this one!

For my parents, who are responsible for getting me into Disney in the first place.
Thank you!

Love,
James
X

Contents

Introduction

Growing up in the 80s and 90s in the north of England with TV choices limited to four channels, my first exposure to Disney came in the form of the animated classics (on very occasional cinema trips and on VHS) and Disney cartoon series—such as *Gummi Bears, Chip 'n Dale Rescue Rangers,* and *Aladdin*—shown on Saturday and Sunday morning kids TV—but I never saw a Disney anthology series. Unlike Richard Rothrock, who writes nostalgically about the role *The Wonderful World of Disney* played in his childhood in *Sunday Nights with Walt* (2017), I have no memories of sitting down with my family to get lost in the dramas and backstage stories of *Disneyland* and its successors, thus such productions inspire no nostalgia in me.

This lack of familiarity with the Disney anthology show or any of the Disney Channel Original Movies (available on cable and satellite channels) growing up, means that I've always experienced such shows and films afresh, as an adult viewer—when I've been able to track them down, that is. For Disney's TV movie output seems a poor cousin to the big screen releases, and even the direct-to-video fare, covered in the first volume of *Disney Connections & Collections.* But *Disneyland* and its successors represent a rich source of comedy and drama, acting and writing debuts, behind the scenes trivia and more.

For this second volume of *Disney Connections & Collections* I wanted to focus on the factual and fictional episodes of the various anthology series, along with the longer-form, sometimes multi-part TV movies that Disney has produced, to discover their connections with the wider world of Disney. From the earliest days of Disney TV in the 1950s and the Davy Crockett phenomenon, right up to the 2018 TV movie adaptation of the *Freaky Friday* stage musical—which was preceded by the original book, the 1976 Disney movie and a 1995 Disney TV movie version—this reference book demonstrates how Disney's approach to TV content has changed over 60 years of broadcasting.

Anthology shows were regularly used to promote Disney's theatrical movies and theme parks, with behind the scenes glimpses at how they were made, as well as providing packages of animated shorts and natural history stories alongside original drama and literary adaptations. Very occasionally, the success of a TV movie would break out into the wider cultural consciousness—witness the fandom and spin-offs that *High School Musical* has wrought—but often these self-contained dramas have passed largely unremarked upon in the Disney literary field, both popular and academic, despite the joy and memories that such productions have brought and continue to bring to audiences both young and young-at-heart.

With Disney soon to launch their new Disney+ streaming service, which aims to rival the likes of Netflix, it will be interesting to see whether more of their anthology and TV movie content is released for modern consumption. Whether that happens or not, you hold in your hands a useful guide to Disney TV movies and anthologies to help you navigate this exciting and somewhat hidden part of the Disney entertainment empire.

How to Use This Book

As with Volume 1, *Disney Connections & Collections: TV Movies & Anthology Shows* is not a book designed to be read all at once. It is a reference work that illustrates the chronological development of Disney's anthology shows and movies made directly for television. You can use it to find out how these shows and movies fit in to the wider world of Disney media, and find out which of these shows are available to view again, in what format, and where to find them.

Compiling this collection has been less straightforward than the previous volume, which considered Disney's theatrical movie output. That is because much more has been written about theatrical movies generally—even beyond Disney, television movies are often overlooked by authors and academics. Television shows and movies do not always receive worldwide releases and are rarely premiered with the same fanfare and promotional blitz as a Hollywood blockbuster.

Disney has been very selective about the television anthology shows or movies that it has released to home media (as you will see in this book), and thus production credits and other information is sometimes hard to find, especially for an independent (British) researcher without access to Disney's archives. This book attempts to fill gaps through cross-checking of sources, but still some information remains elusive.

It would be impossible to include every TV special broadcast on Disney's own television networks, so the entries are restricted to original episodes of Disney's television anthologies and TV movie series. Television broadcasts of theatrically released movies are not included, although compilations of theatrical shorts are included as they often feature new bridging content or animation.

Disney's anthology shows include the following:

- *Disneyland* (1954-1958) ABC
- *Walt Disney Presents* (1958-1961) ABC
- *Walt Disney's Wonderful World of Color* (1961-1969) NBC
- *The Wonderful World of Disney* (1969-1979) NBC
- *Disney's Wonderful World* (1979-1981) NBC
- *Walt Disney* (1981-1983) CBS
- *The Disney Sunday Movie* (1986-1988) ABC

- *The Magical World of Disney* (1988-1990) NBC (1990-1997) Disney Channel
- *The Wonderful World of Disney* (1997-2007) ABC
- Disney Channel Premiere Films (1983-1997) Disney Channel
- Disney Channel Original Movies (1997+) Disney Channel

The entries in this book are arranged chronologically by their earliest US broadcast date, from 1950 to 2019. Included with each entry is the title of the anthology series or brand of which it is a part, as well as details of key production personnel. Details on release dates and approximate running times follow.

The entry then lists other media that have been spun-off from the movie/serial/episode or its characters. In this section, Collections indicates where these spin-offs can be found on home media or in print. This is followed by details regarding the availability of the movie on home media, as well as soundtracks and non-fiction books about the making of the movie. In some cases, a book with a wider focus than the single movie is included where it contains a significant chapter about the movie in question.

The format and layout of each entry is as follows:

Title (Year)
Series title

- **Includes:** If episode is split between two subjects, this is the title of the other subject
- **AKA:** Alternative titles
- **Source:** Details of the book/comic/short story/true story/TV show that inspired the movie/episode
- **Writers:** Names of all credited writers on the movie/episode
- **Director:** Names of all credited directors on the movie/episode
- **Stars:** Names of four lead actors
- **Broadcast:** Date of first broadcast, and the channel it appeared on
- **Length:** Approx. length of movie or parts
- **Comic Strips:** Comic book adaptations
- **Movies:** Spin-offs, including international releases of the movie/episode in question
- **Shorts:** Theatrical, propaganda, direct-to-video (DTV), and educational shorts
- **Stage Musical**: Stage Musical adaptations

- **TV:** TV Series, Anthology or Movie spin-offs, with years of release and channel

- **Theme Parks:** Rides and attractions based on the film or characters at Disney theme parks, including years of operation and park location. Key: Disneyland Resort: Disneyland (DL), Disney California Adventure Park (DCA) Walt Disney World Resort: Magic Kingdom (MK), Disney's Hollywood Studios (HS), Tokyo Disney Resort: Tokyo Disneyland (TDL), Tokyo DisneySea (TDS) Disneyland Paris: Walt Disney Studios Park (WDS)

- **Video:** VHS releases and editions (USA)

- **Video Games**: Amiga, Apple II (AII), Atari ST (AST), Commodore 64 (C64), Game Boy (GB), Game Boy Advance (GBA), Nintendo DS (DS), Nintendo Entertainment System (NES), PC, PlayStation 2 (PS2), PlayStation 3 (PS3), Xbox 360 Games Store (X360S), Wii

- **DVD/Blu-ray:** DVD/Blu-ray releases and editions (USA)

- **Digital:** Availability via Amazon, iTunes, Vudu (USA) Check justwatch.com for up-to-date listings as streaming availability is liable to change—a problem you don't get with physical media! Note that the Disney+ streaming service had not launched at time of writing.

- **Soundtrack:** LP and CD releases and re-releases (and digital-only releases)

- **Books:** Details of publication for non-fiction books relating to the movie or episode.

The information contained in this book has been compiled from official Disney sources as well as other reference books, websites and media consulted by the author (see Further Reading for details). If you are aware of any obvious omissions or inaccuracies, please do let the author know by emailing JamesDoesDisney@outlook.com.

PART ONE

1950–1959

One Hour in Wonderland (1950)

Sponsored by Coca-Cola

Source:
Promo for *Alice in Wonderland* (1951)

Includes:
Clock Cleaners (1937) & *Bone Trouble* (1940)

Writers:
Bill Walsh

Director:
Richard Wallace

Stars:
Walt Disney, Edgar Bergen, Kathy Beaumont, Bobby Driscoll

Broadcast:
Dec 25, 1950, NBC

Length:
59 min

DVD*/Blu-ray:
2004 *Alice in Wonderland: Masterpiece Edition**, 2010 *Alice in Wonderland: Special Un-Anniversary Edition**, 2011 *Alice in Wonderland: 60, Anniversary Edition*

Books:
The Vault of Walt: Volume 7—Christmas Edition (2018) Jim Korkis

The Walt Disney Christmas Show (1951)

Sponsored by Johnson and Johnson

Source:
- Promo for *Peter Pan* (1953)
- Features *The Band Concert* (1935) & *Donald and Pluto* (1936)

Director:
Robert Florey

Stars:
Walt Disney, Kathy Beaumont, Bobby Driscoll

Broadcast:
Dec 25, 1951, NBC

Length:
59 min

Books:
The Vault of Walt: Volume 7—Christmas Edition (2018) Jim Korkis

The Disneyland Story (1954)

Disneyland

AKA:
What Is Disneyland?

Includes:
A Tribute to Mickey Mouse

Source:
Behind the scenes of Disneyland

Director:
Robert Florey

Broadcast:
Oct 27, 1954, ABC

Length:
54 min

TV Anthology:
The Pre-Opening Report on Disneyland (1955) Includes *A Tribute to Mickey Mouse*

DVD:
2001 *WD Treasures: Disneyland, USA*

Prairie (1954)

Disneyland (½ episode)

Includes:
Seal Island (1948)

Source:
Behind the scenes of *The Vanishing Prairie* (1954)

Directors:
James Algar, Richard Bare

Broadcast:
Nov 10, 1954, ABC

Length:
23 min

DVD:
2006 WD Legacy Collection: True-Life Adventures Vol 2—Lands of Exploration

Books:
True-Life Adventures: A History of Walt Disney's Nature Documentaries (2017) Christian Moran

The Donald Duck Story (1954)

Disneyland

AKA:
The Story of Donald Duck

Includes:
Orphan's Benefit (1941), *Honey Harvester* (1949), *Tea for Two Hundred* (1948), *Donald's Dream Voice* (1948), *Three for Breakfast* (1948)

Writers:
Ted Berman, Al Bertino, Jack Hannah

Directors:
Jack Hannah, Robert Florey

Broadcast:
Nov 17, 1954, ABC

Length:
54 min

A Story of Dogs (1954)

Disneyland

Source:
Behind the scenes of *Lady and the Tramp* (1955)

Includes:
Beach Picnic (1939), *Lend a Paw* (1941), *The Legend of Coyote Rock* (1945)

Writers:
Clyde Geronimi, Tom Adair, Erdman Penner

Directors:
Clyde Geronimi, C. August Nichols, Robert Florey

Broadcast:
Dec 1, 1954, ABC

Length:
54 min

DVD*/Blu-ray:
2004 *WD Treasures: The Complete Pluto Vol 1** (29 min excerpt), 2006 *Lady and the Tramp: Platinum Edition** (17 min excerpt), 2012 *Lady and the Tramp: Diamond Edition* (17 min excerpt)

Operation Undersea (1954)

Disneyland

Source:
Behind the scenes of *20,000 Leagues Under the Sea* (1954)

Writers:
Winston Hibler, John Meredyth Lucas, Ted Sears

Directors:
Winston Hibler, Hamilton Luske

Stars:
Walt Disney, Winston Hibler, Kirk Douglas, Richard Fleischer

Broadcast:
Dec 8, 1954, ABC

Length:
52 min

TV Anthology:
Pacifically Peeking (1968) Features edited content

DVD:
2003 *20,000 Leagues Under the Sea: Special Edition* (7 min excerpt)

Digital:
Amazon, iTunes

Davy Crockett: Indian Fighter (1954)

Disneyland

Source:
Based on the life of Davy Crockett

Writers:
Tom Blackburn

Director:
Norman Foster

Stars:
Fess Parker, Buddy Ebsen, Basil Rusydael, William Bakewell

Broadcast:
Dec 15, 1954, ABC
Length:
54 min
Comic Strips:
Davy Crockett Indian Fighter (Four Color Comics #631, May 1955)
Movies:
- *Davy Crockett: King of the Wild Frontier* (1955) Episode edited into film
- *Davy Crockett and the River Pirates* (1956) Midquel

TV Anthology:
- *Davy Crockett: Indian Fighter* (1955)
- *Davy Crockett Goes to Congress* (1955)
- *Davy Crockett at the Alamo* (1955)
- *Davy Crockett's Keelboat Race* (1955)
- *Davy Crockett and the River Pirates* (1955)
- *Davy Crockett: Rainbow in the Thunder* (1988)
- *Davy Crockett: A Natural Man* (1988)
- *Davy Crockett: Guardian Spirit* (1989)
- *Davy Crockett: A Letter to Polly* (1989)
- *Davy Crockett: Warrior's Farewell* (1989)

Theme Parks:
- Davy Crockett Museum (DL 1955-1956)
- Davy Crockett Explorer Canoes (DL 1956+), (MK 1971-1994)

DVD:
2001 *WD Treasures: Davy Crockett: The Complete Televised Series*
Books:
- *The Disney Live-Action Productions/Walt Disney and Live Action* (1994/2016) John G. West
- *The Davy Crockett Craze* (1996) Paul F. Anderson

Cameras in Africa (1954)

Disneyland (½ episode)
Includes:
Beaver Valley (1950)
Source:
Behind the scenes of *The African Lion* (1955)

Writers:
Winston Hibler, Ted Sears, Lawrence Edward Watkin, Jack Speirs

Directors:
Winston Hibler, James Algar

Broadcast:
Dec 29, 1954, ABC

Length:
20 min

DVD:
2006 *WD Legacy Collection: True-Life Adventures Vol 3—Creatures of the Wild*

Books:
True-Life Adventures: A History of Walt Disney's Nature Documentaries (2017) Christian Moran

Monsters of the Deep (1955)

Disneyland

Source:
Includes behind the scenes of *20,000 Leagues Under the Sea* (1954)

Writers:
Winston Hibler, John Meredyth Lucas, Ted Sears, Jack Speirs

Directors:
Peter Godfrey, Hamilton Luske

Broadcast:
Jan 19, 1955, ABC

Length:
54 min

DVD:
2003 *20,000 Leagues Under the Sea: Special Edition* (7 min excerpt)

Davy Crockett Goes to Congress (1955)

Disneyland

Source:
Davy Crockett #2

Writers:
Tom Blackburn

Director:
Norman Foster

Stars:
Fess Parker, Basil Ruysdael, William Bakewell, Mike Mazurki

Broadcast:
Jan 26, 1955, ABC

Length:
53 min

Comic Strips:
Davy Crockett Goes to Washington (Walt Disney's Davy Crockett: King of the Wild Frontier, Sep 1955)

Movies:
Davy Crockett: King of the Wild Frontier (1955) Episode edited into film

DVD:
2001 *WD Treasures: Davy Crockett: The Complete Televised Series*

Books:
- *The Disney Live-Action Productions/Walt Disney and Live Action* (1994/2016) John G. West
- *The Davy Crockett Craze* (1996) Paul F. Anderson

A Progress Report (1955)

Disneyland (½ episode)

Includes:
Nature's Half Acre (1951)

Source:
Behind the scenes of Disneyland

Director:
Al Teeter

Broadcast:
Feb 9, 1955, ABC

Length:
19 min

Books:
True-Life Adventures: A History of Walt Disney's Nature Documentaries (2017) Christian Moran

Cavalcade of Songs (1955)

Disneyland

Source:
Behind the scenes of *Lady and the Tramp* (1955)

Includes:
Three Little Pigs (1933)

Writers:
Erdman Penner, Joe Rinaldi

Director:
Wilfred Jackson, Peter Godfrey

Broadcast:
Feb 16, 1955, ABC

Length:
52 min

DVD*/Blu-ray:
2006 *Lady and the Tramp: Platinum Edition** (22 min excerpt), 2012 *Lady and the Tramp: Diamond Edition* (22 min excerpt)

Davy Crockett at the Alamo (1955)

Disneyland

Source:
Davy Crockett #3

Writers:
Tom Blackburn

Director:
Norman Foster

Stars:
Fess Parker, Buddy Ebsen, Hans Conried, Kenneth Tobey

Broadcast:
Feb 23, 1955, ABC

Length:
53 min

Comic Strips:
Davy Crockett at the Alamo (Four Color #639, Jul 1955)

Movies:
Davy Crockett: King of the Wild Frontier (1955) Episode edited into film

DVD:
2001 *WD Treasures: Davy Crockett: The Complete Televised Series*

Books:
- *The Disney Live-Action Productions/Walt Disney and Live Action* (1994/2016) John G. West
- *The Davy Crockett Craze* (1996) Paul F. Anderson

From Aesop to Hans Christian Andersen (1955)

Disneyland

Includes:

The Tortoise and the Hare (1935), *Brave Little Tailor* (1938), *The Ugly Duckling* (1939)

Writers:

Bill Peet

Director:

Clyde Geronimi

Broadcast:

Mar 2, 1955, ABC

Length:

54 min

Movies:

From Aesop to Hans Christian Andersen (1957, UK) (1959, Denmark) (1960, Japan)

Man in Space (1955)

Disneyland

Writers:

Ward Kimball, William Bosche

Director:

Ward Kimball

Broadcast:

Mar 9, 1955, ABC

Length:

51 min (Original), 33 min (Theatrical)

Comic Strips:

Man in Space: A Science Feature from Tomorrowland (Four Color #716, Aug 1956)

Shorts:

- *Man in Space* (1956) (1957, Japan/Denmark)
- *All About Weightlessness* (1964) Educational

DVD:

2004 *WD Treasures: Tomorrowland*

Books:

The Walt Disney Film Archives: The Animated Movies 1921-1968 (2016) Ed. Daniel Kothenschulte

A Further Report on Disneyland (1955)

Disneyland (½ episode)

AKA:
A/The Pre-Opening Report from Disneyland

Includes:
A Tribute to Mickey Mouse (1954, originally from *The Disneyland Story*)

Source:
Behind the scenes of Disneyland

Writers:
Lee Chaney, Milton M. Raison

Director:
Wilfred Jackson

Broadcast:
Jul 13, 1955, ABC

Length:
24 min

Dateline: Disneyland (1955)

Source:
Live opening of Disneyland

Writers:
Milton Raison

Directors:
Stuart Phelps, John Rich

Stars:
Art Linkletter, Bob Cummings, Ronald Reagan

Broadcast:
Jul 17, 1955, ABC

Length:
76 min

DVD:
2001 *WD Treasures: Disneyland USA*

Behind the True-Life Cameras (1955)

Disneyland (½ episode)

Includes:
Olympic Elk (1952)

Source:
Behind the scenes of *Secrets of Life* (1956) and *The African Lion* (1955)

Writers:
Jack Speirs, Ted Sears, Winston Hibler

Director:
Winston Hibler

Broadcast:
Sep 21, 1955, ABC

Length:
24 min

DVD:
2006 WD Legacy Collection: True-Life Adventures Vol 2—Lands of Exploration

Books:
True-Life Adventures: A History of Walt Disney's Nature Documentaries (2017) Christian Moran

People and Places: Tiburon (1955)

Disneyland (½ episode)

Includes:
Excerpts from *Men Against the Arctic* (1955), *Sardinia* (1956), *The Blue Men of Morocco* (1957)

AKA:
People and Places: Tiburon, Sardinia, Morocco, Icebreakers

Source:
Unreleased People and Places short

Director:
Winston Hibler

Broadcast:
Oct 5, 1955, ABC

Length:
? min

The Adventures of Mickey Mouse (1955)

Disneyland

AKA:
Mickey's Greatest Adventures (1980), *Adventures with Mickey*

Includes:
The Band Concert (1935), *Alpine Climbers* (1936), *Squatter's Rights* (1946), *Mickey and the Beanstalk* (1947)

Director:
Jack Hannah, Bill Roberts

Broadcast:
Oct 12, 1955, ABC

Length:
52 min

The Story of the Silly Symphony (1955)

Disneyland

Includes:
Flowers and Trees (1932), *Little Hiawatha* (1937)

Writers:
Bill Peet

Director:
Clyde Geronimi

Broadcast:
Oct 19, 1955, ABC

Length:
52 min

Davy Crockett's Keelboat Race (1955)

Disneyland

Source:
Davy Crockett #4

Writers:
Tom Blackburn, Norman Foster

Director:
Norman Foster

Stars:
Fess Parker, Buddy Ebsen, Jeff York, Kenneth Tobey

Broadcast:
Nov 16, 1955, ABC

Length:
54 min

Movies:
Davy Crockett and the River Boat Pirates (1956) Episode edited into film

DVD:
2001 *WD Treasures: Davy Crockett—The Complete Televised Series*

Books:
- *The Disney Live-Action Productions/Walt Disney and Live Action* (1994/2016) John G. West
- *The Davy Crockett Craze* (1996) Paul F. Anderson

The Story of the Animated Drawing (1955)
Disneyland

Writers:
Dick Huemer, McLaren Stewart

Director:
Wilfred Jackson, William Beaudine

Broadcast:
Nov 30, 1955, ABC

Length:
52 min

Shorts:
The History of Animation (1975) Educational, abridged

DVD:
2002 *WD Treasures: Behind The Scenes at the Walt Disney Studio*

Digital:
Vudu

The Goofy Success Story (1955)
Disneyland

Includes:
Moving Day (1936), *Moose Hunters* (1937), *How to Ride a Horse* (1941/50), *Motor Mania* (1950)

Writers:
Jack Kinney

Director:
Jack Kinney

Broadcast:
Dec 7, 1955, ABC

Length:
52 min

Comic Strips:
Goofy Success Story (Four Color #702, May 1956)

Shorts:
The Goofy Success Story (1959, International)

DVD:
2000 *A Goofy Movie*

Davy Crockett and the River Pirates (1955)

Disneyland

Source:
Davy Crockett #5

Writers:
Tom Blackburn, Norman Foster

Director:
Norman Foster

Stars:
Fess Parker, Buddy Ebsen, Jeff York, Kenneth Tobey

Broadcast:
Dec 14, 1955, ABC

Length:
54 min

Comic Books:
Davy Crockett and the River Pirates (Four Color #671, Dec 1955)

Movies:
Davy Crockett and the River Boat Pirates (1956) Episode edited into film

DVD:
2001 *WD Treasures: Davy Crockett: The Complete Televised Series*

Books:
- *The Disney Live-Action Productions/Walt Disney and Live Action* (1994/2016) John G. West
- *The Davy Crockett Craze* (1996) Paul F. Anderson

Man and the Moon (1955)

Disneyland

AKA:
Tomorrow the Moon (1959)

Writers:
William Bosche, John W. Dunn, Ward Kimball

Director:
Ward Kimball

Broadcast:
Dec 28, 1955, ABC

Length:
53 min

Shorts:
Man and the Moon (International)

DVD:
2004 *WD Treasures: Tomorrowland*

Books:
The Walt Disney Film Archives: The Animated Movies 1921-1968 (2016)
Ed. Daniel Kothenschulte

The Mickey Mouse Club Serials: Season One (1955–1956)

THE ADVENTURES OF SPIN AND MARTY

Source:
Marty Markham (1942) Lawrence E. Watkin

Director:
William Beaudine

Stars:
David Stollery, Tim Considine, Roy Barcroft, Harry Carey Jr.

Broadcast:
Nov 7—Dec 9, 1955, ABC x 25 episodes

Length:
11 min

Comic Strips:
Spin and Marty (Four Color #714, 767, 808, 826, Spin and Marty #5-9, Four Color #1026, 1082, Jun 1956—May 1960)

TV Movies:
- *Spin and Marty: The Movie* (1995) Edited from episodes
- *The New Adventures of Spin and Marty: Suspect Behavior* (2000) Remake

TV Serials:
- *The Further Adventures of Spin and Marty* (1956)

- *The New Adventures of Spin and Marty* (1957)

DVD:
2005 *WD Treasures: The Adventures of Spin & Marty*

BORDER COLLIE

Director:
Larry Lansburgh

Stars:
Bobby Evans, Arthur N. Allen

Broadcast:
ABC x 4 episodes

CORKY AND WHITE SHADOW

Director:
William Beaudine

Stars:
Darlene Gillespie, Buddy Ebsen, Lloyd Corrigan

Broadcast:
ABC x 18 episodes

SAN JUAN RIVER EXPEDITION

Director:
Al Teeter

Broadcast:
ABC x 5 episodes

WHAT I WANT TO BE

Broadcast:
Oct 3—Oct 14, 1955, ABC x 10 episodes

A Tribute to Joel Chandler Harris (1956)

Disneyland

Director:
William Beaudine, Clyde Geronimi

Broadcast:
Jan 18, 1956, ABC

Length:
52 min

A Day in the Life of Donald Duck (1956)

Disneyland

Includes:

Good Scouts (1938), *Fire Chief* (1940), *The Vanishing Private* (1942), *Drip Dippy Donald* (1948)

Writers:

Al Bertino, David Detiege

Director:

Jack Hannah

Broadcast:

Feb 1, 1956, ABC

Length:

49 min

DVD:

2005 *WD Treasures: The Chronological Donald Vol 2*

Survival in Nature (1956)

Disneyland

Source:

Edited from True-Life Adventures subjects

Director:

Winston Hibler

Broadcast:

Feb 8, 1956, ABC

Length:

52 min

Books:

True-Life Adventures: A History of Walt Disney's Nature Documentaries (2017) Christian Moran

Our Unsung Villains (1956)

Disneyland

Writers:

Carl Cons, Hamilton S. Luske

Director:

Hamilton S. Luske, Wilfred Jackson

Broadcast:

Feb 15, 1956, ABC

Length:
52 min

A Trip Thru Adventureland (1956)

Disneyland (½ episode)

Includes:
Water Birds (1952)

Source:
Behind the scenes of Disneyland

Director:
Winston Hibler

Broadcast:
Feb 29, 1956, ABC

Length:
20 min

On Vacation (1956)

Disneyland

AKA:
On Vacation with Mickey Mouse and Friends

Includes:
Hawaiian Holiday (1937), *Mickey's Trailer* (1938), *Goofy and Wilbur* (1939), *Canine Caddy* (1941), *Bubble Bee* (1949), *Dude Duck* (1951)

Director:
Jack Hannah

Broadcast:
Mar 7, 1956, ABC

Length:
52 min

DiscoVision:
1979 *On Vacation with Mickey Mouse and Friends*

Video:
1981 *On Vacation with Mickey Mouse and Friends*

The Goofy Sports Story (1956)

Disneyland

Includes:
The Art of Skiing (1941), *How to Play Baseball* (1942), *The Olympic Champ* (1942), *How to Play Football* (1944), *Goofy Gymnastics* (1949), *Football Now and Then* (1953)

Writers:
Jack Kinney
Director:
Jack Kinney
Broadcast:
Mar 21, 1956, ABC
Length:
52 min
Shorts:
The Goofy Sports Story (1957, UK) (1964, International)
TV Movies:
Superstar Goofy (DTV 1972 Europe, 1976 US) Edited into feature

Where Do the Stories Come From? (1956)

Disneyland
Includes:
Donald Gets Drafted (1942), *Fall Out—Fall In* (1943), *Crazy Over Daisy* (1950), *R'coon Dawg* (1951), *Out of Scale* (1951)
Writers:
Bil Berg, Al Bertino, Dave Detiege, Roy Williams, Ralph Wright
Director:
Jack Hannah
Broadcast:
Apr 4, 1956, ABC
Length:
52 min
DVD:
2006 *WD Treasures: Your Host, Walt Disney*

Behind the Scenes with Fess Parker (1956)

Disneyland
Source:
Behind the scenes of *The Great Locomotive Chase* (1956)
Writers:
James Algar, Dwight V. BABCock, Lawrence Edward Watkin
Director:
Francis D. Lyon
Stars:
Fess Parker

Broadcast:
May 30, 1956, ABC

Length:
52 min

Antarctica—Past and Present (1956)

Disneyland

Writers:
Winston Hibler, Ted Sears, Jack Speirs

Director:
Winston Hibler

Broadcast:
Sep 12, 1956, ABC

Length:
52 min

Shorts:
Seven Cities of Antarctica (1958) Edited from TV episode

The Great Cat Family (1956)

Disneyland

Includes:
Lambert the Sheepish Lion (1952)

Writers:
Winston Hibler, Bill Peet, Ted Sears

Director:
Clyde Geronimi

Broadcast:
Sep 19, 1956, ABC

Length:
52 min

Comic Strips:
The Great Cat Family (Four Color #750, Nov 1956)

DVD*/Blu-ray:
2008*/2012 *The Aristocats: Special Edition* (13 min excerpt)

Searching for Nature's Mysteries (1956)

Disneyland

Source:
Behind the scenes of *Secrets of Life* (1956)

Writers:
Dwight Hauser
Director:
Winston Hibler
Broadcast:
Sep 26, 1956, ABC
Length:
52 min
DVD:
2006 *WD Legacy Collection: True-Life Adventures Vol 4—Nature's Mysteries*
Books:
True-Life Adventures: A History of Walt Disney's Nature Documentaries (2017) Christian Moran

Goofy's Cavalcade of Sports (1956)

Disneyland
Includes:
The Art of Self Defense (1941), *How to Fish* (1942), *How to Swim* (1942), *How to Play Golf* (1944), *Double Dribble* (1946)
Director:
Wolfgang Reitherman
Broadcast:
Oct 17, 1956, ABC
Length:
52 min
TV Movies:
Superstar Goofy (DTV 1972 Europe, 1976 US) Edited into feature

Behind the Cameras at Lapland (1956)

Disneyland (½ episode)
Includes:
The Alaskan Eskimo (1953)
Source:
Behind the scenes of *Lapland* (1957)
Director:
Winston Hibler, James Algar
Broadcast:
Oct 24, 1956, ABC

Length:
23 min

The Plausible Impossible (1956)

Disneyland

Writers:
Dick Huemer

Directors:
William Beaudine, Wilfred Jackson

Broadcast:
Oct 31, 1956, ABC

Length:
52 min

DVD:
2002 *WD Treasures: Behind The Scenes at the Walt Disney Studio*

Digital:
Amazon, Vudu

Cameras in Samoa (1956)

Disneyland (½ episode)

Includes:
The Holland Story

Source:
Behind the scenes of *Samoa* (1956)

Director:
Winston Hibler

Broadcast:
Nov 7, 1956, ABC

Length:
25 min

The Holland Story (1956)

Disneyland (½ episode)

Includes:
Cameras in Samoa

Director:
Winston Hibler

Broadcast:
Nov 7, 1956, ABC

Length:
25 min

Along the Oregon Trail (1956)

Disneyland

Source:
Behind the scenes of *Westward Ho, the Wagons!* (1956)

Director:
William Beaudine

Broadcast:
Nov 14, 1956, ABC

Length:
52 min

At Home with Donald Duck (1956)

Disneyland

AKA:
Happy Birthday Donald Duck (1976)

Includes:
Foul Hunting (1947), *Pluto's Blue Note* (1947), *Mickey and the Seal* (1948), *Donald's Happy Birthday* (1949), *Sea Salts* (1949)

Director:
Jack Hannah

Broadcast:
Nov 21, 1956, ABC

Length:
52 min

DiscoVision:
1979

Pluto's Day (1956)

Disneyland

Includes:
Mother Pluto (1936), *Bone Trouble* (1940), *Pluto's Dream House* (1940), *Pluto's Playmate* (1941), *A Gentleman's Gentleman* (1941), *Pluto and the Armadillo* (1943), *Food for Feudin'* (1950), *The Simple Things* (1953)

Director:
Wolfgang Reitherman

Broadcast:
Dec 12, 1956, ABC

Length:
52 min

The Mickey Mouse Club Serials: Season Two (1956-1957)

ADVENTURE IN DAIRYLAND

AKA:
The Dairy Story, Adventures In Dairyland

Director:
William Beaudine

Stars:
Annette Funicello, Sammy Ogg, Kevin Cororan

Broadcast:
ABC x 8 episodes

THE BOYS OF THE WESTERN SEA

Stars:
Kjeld Bentzen, Anne Grete Hilding, Lars Henning-Jensen, Nette Hoj Hansen

Broadcast:
ABC x 8 episodes

THE FIRST AMERICANS

Stars:
Tony Nakina, Iron Eyes Cody

Broadcast:
ABC x 4 episodes

THE FURTHER ADVENTURES OF SPIN AND MARTY

Source:
Sequel to *The Adventures of Spin and Marty* (1955-1956 season)

Director:
William Beaudine

Stars:
Tim Considine, David Stollery, Annette Funicello, B.G. Norman

Broadcast:
ABC x 23 episodes

Length:
11 min

THE HARDY BOYS: THE MYSTERY OF THE APPLEGATE TREASURE

Source:
The Hardy Boys (1927+) Franklin W. Dixon

Writer:
Jackson Gillis

Director:
Charles Haas

Stars:
Tim Considine, Tommy Kirk, Carole Ann Campbell, Donald MacDonald

Broadcast:
Oct 1—26, 1956, ABC x 20 episodes

Length:
12 min

Comic Strips:
The Hardy Boys (Four Color #760, Dec 1956)

TV Serial:
The Hardy Boys: The Mystery of Ghost Farm (1956-1957 season)

DVD:
2006 WD Treasures: The Hardy Boys, 2014 Collector's Edition

THE SECRET OF MYSTERY LAKE

Director:
Larry Lansburgh

Stars:
George Fenneman, Gloria Marshall, Bogue Bell, R.P. Alexander

Broadcast:
ABC x 7 episodes

Your Host, Donald Duck (1957)

Disneyland

Includes:
The Whale Who Wanted to Sing at the Met (1946/1954), Timber (1941), Clown of the Jungle (1947), Test Pilot Donald (1951), Uncle Donald's Ants (1952)

Writers:
Bill Berg, Al Bertino, Dave Detiege, Ray Patin

Director:
Jack Hannah

Broadcast:
Jan 16, 1957, ABC

Length:
52 min

Our Friend the Atom (1957)

Disneyland

Writers:
Milt Banta

Director:
Hamilton Luske

Broadcast:
Jan 23, 1957, ABC

Length:
52 min

Shorts:
The Atom: A Closer Look (1980) Educational, updated version

DVD:
2004 *WD Treasures: Tomorrowland*

All About Magic (1957)

Disneyland

Includes:
Magician Mickey (1937), *Trick or Treat* (1952)

Writers:
Milt Banta, Erdman Penner, Perce Pearce, Ralph Wright

Director:
Hamilton Luske

Broadcast:
Jan 30, 1957, ABC

Length:
52 min

DVD*/Blu-ray:
2001 *The Sword in the Stone: Gold Classic Collection** (36 min excerpt),
2008 *The Sword in the Stone: 45th, Anniversary Edition** (7 min excerpt),
2013 *The Sword in the Stone: 50th, Anniversary Edition* (7 min excerpt)

Tricks of Our Trade (1957)

Disneyland

Writers:
Dick Huemer

Director:
Wilfred Jackson

Broadcast:
Feb 13, 1957, ABC

Length:
52 min

Shorts:
Tricks of Our Trade (?) Educational, edited

DVD:
2002 *WD Treasures: Behind the Scenes at the Walt Disney Studios*

Digital:
Vudu

The Crisler Story (1957)

Disneyland (½ episode)

Includes:
Prowlers of the Everglades (1953)

Source:
Behind the scenes of *White Wilderness* (1958)

Writer:
Dwight Hauser

Director:
James Algar

Broadcast:
Feb 27, 1957, ABC

Length:
19 min

DVD:
2006 *WD Legacy Collection: True-Life Adventures Vol 1—Wonders of the World*

Books:
True-Life Adventures: A History of Walt Disney's Nature Documentaries (2017) Christian Moran

Man in Flight (1957)

Disneyland

Includes:
Footage from *Victory Through Air Power* (1943)

Writers:
Milt Banta, Heinz Haber

Director:
Hamilton Luske

Broadcast:
Mar 6, 1957, ABC

Length:
52 min

Comic Strips:
Man in Flight (Four Color #836, Sep 1957)

Shorts:
1958 (International)

TV Anthology:
1961 Edited version

The Adventure Story (1957)

Disneyland

AKA:
The Goofy Adventure Story

Includes:
The Whalers (1938), *Tugboat Mickey* (1940), *How to Be a Sailor* (1944), *Tiger Trouble* (1945), *African Diary* (1945), *Californy er Bust* (1945), *A Knight for a Day* (1946), *No Smoking* (1950), *Father's Lion* (1952), *For Whom the Bulls Toil* (1953)

Writers:
Dick Kinney, Brice Mack, Bill Peet

Director:
Wolfgang Reitherman

Broadcast:
Mar 20, 1957, ABC

Length:
52 min

Comic Strips:
The Goofy Adventure Story (Four Color #857, Nov 1957)

Donald's Award (1957)

Disneyland

Includes:

Trombone Trouble (1944), *The Eyes Have It* (1945), *Cured Duck* (1945), *Out on a Limb* (1950), *Bee on Guard* (1951)

Writers:

Bill Berg, Al Bertino, Dave Detiege, Nick George, Roy Williams

Director:

Jack Hannah

Broadcast:

Mar 27, 1957, ABC

Length:

52 min

Disneyland, The Park (1957)

Disneyland (½ episode)

Includes:

Pecos Bill (1948/1955)

Source:

Behind the scenes of Disneyland

Writers:

Larry Clemmons

Directors:

Hamilton Luske, Clyde Geronimi

Broadcast:

Apr 3, 1957, ABC

Length:

25 min

More About the Silly Symphonies (1957)

Disneyland

Source:

Sequel to *The Story of the Silly Symphony* (1955)

Includes:

Merbabies (1938), *The Grasshopper and the Ants* (1934), *Farmyard Symphony* (1938), *Who Killed Cock Robin?* (1935), *Wynken, Blynken and Nod* (1938)

Writers:

Nick George, Bill Berg

Director:
Clyde Geronimi

Broadcast:
Apr 17, 1957, ABC

Length:
52 min

The Yellowstone Story (1957)

Disneyland (½ episode)

Includes:
Bear Country (1953)

Source:
Behind the scenes of *Bear Country* (1953)

Writers:
James Algar, Lee Chaney

Director:
James Algar

Broadcast:
May 1, 1957, ABC

Length:
17 min

DVD:
2006 *WD Legacy Collection: True-Life Adventures Vol 3—Creatures of the Wild*

Books:
True-Life Adventures: A History of Walt Disney's Nature Documentaries (2017) Christian Moran

The Liberty Story (1957)

Disneyland

Includes:
Ben and Me (1953)

Source:
Behind the scenes / excerpt of *Johnny Tremain* (1957)

Writers:
James Algar

Director:
Hamilton S. Luske, Robert Stevenson

Broadcast:
May 29, 1957, ABC
Length:
48 min
DVD:
2005 *Johnny Tremain* (22 min excerpt)
Digital:
Amazon

Antarctica: Operation Deep Freeze (1957)

Disneyland
Writers:
Winston Hibler
Director:
Winston Hibler
Broadcast:
Jun 5, 1957, ABC
Length:
54 min
Shorts:
Seven Cities of Antarctica (1958) Edited from TV episode
Book:
Operation Deepfreeze (1957) Rear Admiral George J. Dufek

The Fourth Anniversary Show (1957)

Disneyland
Includes:
Peter and the Wolf (1946/1955)
Writers:
Albert Duffy
Director:
Sidney Miller
Broadcast:
Sep 11, 1957, ABC
Length:
52 min
DVD:
2006 *WD Treasures: Your Host, Walt Disney*

Four Fabulous Characters (1957)

Disneyland

Includes:
Casey at the Bat (1946), *The Martins and the Coys* (1946), *The Legend of Johnny Appleseed* (1948), *The Brave Engineer* (1950)

Writers:
Homer Brightman

Director:
Hamilton S. Luske

Broadcast:
Sep 18, 1957, ABC

Length:
52 min

Adventure in Wildwood Heart (1957)

Disneyland

Source:
Behind the scenes of *Perri* (1957)

Writers:
Jack Speirs, Winston Hibler

Director:
Hamilton S. Luske

Broadcast:
Sep 25, 1957, ABC

Length:
49 min

DVD:
2006 *WD Legacy Collection: True-Life Adventures Vol 4—Nature's Mysteries*

Books:
True-Life Adventures: A History of Walt Disney's Nature Documentaries (2017) Christian Moran

The Saga of Andy Burnett: Andy's Initiation (1957)

Disneyland

Source:
The Saga of Andy Burnett (1930-1942) Stewart Edward White

Writers:

Thomas W. Blackburn

Director:

Lewis R. Foster

Stars:

Jerome Courtland, Jeff York, Andrew Duggan, Slim Pickens

Broadcast:

Oct 2, 1957, ABC

Length:

54 min

Comic Strips:

Walt Disney's Andy Burnett (Four Color #865, Dec 1957)

TV Anthology:

- *The Saga of Andy Burnett: Andy's First Chore* (1957)
- *The Saga of Andy Burnett: Andy's Love Affair* (1957)
- *The Saga of Andy Burnett: The Land of Enemies* (1958)
- *The Saga of Andy Burnett: White Man's Medicine* (1958)
- *The Saga of Andy Burnett: The Big Council* (1958)

Book:

The Disney Live-Action Productions/Walt Disney and Live Action (1994/2016) John G. West

The Saga of Andy Burnett: Andy's First Chore (1957)

Disneyland

Source:

The Saga of Andy Burnett #2

Writers:

Thomas W. Blackburn

Director:

Lewis R. Foster

Stars:

Jerome Courtland, Jeff York, Andrew Duggan, Slim Pickens

Broadcast:

Oct 9, 1957, ABC

Length:

54 min

The Saga of Andy Burnett: Andy's Love Affair (1957)

Disneyland

Source:
The Saga of Andy Burnett #3

Writers:
Thomas W. Blackburn

Director:
Lewis R. Foster

Stars:
Jerome Courtland, Jeff York, Andrew Duggan, Slim Pickens

Broadcast:
Oct 16, 1957, ABC

Length:
54 min

Duck for Hire (1957)

Disneyland

Includes:
Truant Officer Donald (1941), *Bellboy Donald* (1942), *Lighthouse Keeping* (1946), *Straight Shooters* (1947), *All in a Nutshell* (1949), *Lucky Number* (1951)

Writers:
Al Bertino, Nick George, David Detiege, Bill Berg

Director:
Jack Hannah

Broadcast:
Oct 23, 1957, ABC

Length:
54 min (Original), 30 min (1982 repeat)

Adventures in Fantasy (1957)

Disneyland

Includes:
Johnnie Fedora and Alice Bluebonnet (1946), *Little Toot* (1948), *Susie the Little Blue Coupe* (1952), *The Little House* (1952)

Writers:
Bill Cottrell, Bill Peet, Erdman Penner

Director:
Bill Justice
Broadcast:
Nov 6, 1957, ABC
Length:
54 min

To the South Pole for Science (1957)

Disneyland
Writers:
Winston Hibler
Director:
Winston Hibler
Broadcast:
Nov 13, 1957, ABC
Length:
54 min
Shorts:
Seven Cities of Antarctica (1958) Edited from TV episode

The Best Doggoned Dog in the World (1957)

Disneyland
Includes:
Arizona Sheepdog (1955)
Source:
Behind the scenes of *Old Yeller* (1957)
Writers:
James Algar, Lee Chaney
Director:
Robert Stevenson
Broadcast:
Nov 20, 1957, ABC
Length:
52 min
DVD:
2002 *Old Yeller: Vault Disney Collection*, 2005 *Old Yeller: 2-Movie Collection*
Blu-ray:
2015 *One Hundred and One Dalmatians: Diamond Edition* (1961 version)

How to Relax (1957)

Disneyland

Source:
Excerpts of various Goofy shorts (1937-1952)

Writers:
Bill Berg, Al Bertino, Albert Duffy, Dick Dinney, Milt Schaffer

Director:
Wolfgang Reitherman

Broadcast:
Nov 27, 1957, ABC

Length:
54 min

Mars and Beyond (1957)

Disneyland

Writers:
William Bosche, John W. Dunn, Charles Downs, Con Pederson, Ward Kimball

Director:
Ward Kimball

Broadcast:
Dec 4, 1957, ABC

Length:
53 min (Original), 49 mins (Theatrical)

Comic Strips:
Mars and Beyond (Four Color #866, Dec 1957)

Shorts:
- *Mars and Beyond* (1957)
- *Cosmic Capers* (1979) Edited

DVD*/Blu-ray:
2004 *WD Treasures: Tomorrowland**, 2007 *Roving Mars*

Books:
The Walt Disney Film Archives: The Animated Movies 1921-1968 (2016) Ed. Daniel Kothenschulte

The Horse of the West (1957)

Disneyland

Writers:
Janet Lansburgh

Director:
Larry Lansburgh
Narrator:
Rex Allen
Broadcast:
Dec 11, 1957, ABC
Length:
53 min

The Mickey Mouse Club Serials: Season Three (1957-1958)

THE ADVENTURES OF CLINT AND MAC

Director:
Terrence Fisher
Stars:
Neil Wolfe, Jonathan Bailey, Sandra Michaels, John Warwick
Broadcast:
Dec 30, 1957—Jan 17, 1958, ABC x 15 episodes

ANNETTE

Source:
Margaret (1950) Janette Sebring Lowrey
Writers:
Lillie Hayward
Director:
Charles Lamont
Stars:
Annette Funicello, Tim Considine, David Stollery, Judy Nugent
Broadcast:
Feb 10—Mar 7, 1958, ABC x 20 episodes
Length:
10 min
Comic Strips:
Annette (Four Color #905, May 1958)
Annette's Life Story (Four Color #1100, May-Jul 1960)
DVD:
2008 *WD Treasures: The Mickey Mouse Club Presents Annette*

*T*HE HARDY BOYS: THE MYSTERY OF GHOST FARM

Source:
The Hardy Boys (1927+) Franklin W. Dixon; follows *The Hardy Boys: The Mystery of the Applegate Treasure* (1956)

Writers:
Jackson Gillis

Director:
Robert Springsteen

Stars:
Tim Considine, Tommy Kirk, Carole Ann Campbell, Sarah Selby

Broadcast:
1957-1958, ABC x 15 episodes

Comic Strips:
The Hardy Boys: The Mystery of Ghost Farm (Four Color #887, Jan 1958)

THE NEW ADVENTURES OF SPIN AND MARTY

Source:
Sequel to *The Adventures of Spin and Marty* (1955-1956 season)

Director:
Charles Barton

Stars:
Tim Considine, David Stollery, Kevin Corcoran, Annette Funicello

Broadcast:
1957-1958, ABC x 30 episodes

Comic Strips:
Spin and Marty and Annette (Four Color #826, Sep 1957)

Faraway Places: High, Hot and Wet (1958)

Disneyland

Includes:
Siam (1954)

Source:
Behind the scenes of People & Places

Broadcast:
Jan 1, 1958, ABC

Length:
53 min

Donald's Weekend (1958)

Disneyland

Includes:

Donald's Golf Game (1938), *Mr. Duck Steps Out* (1940), *Early to Bed* (1941), *Donald's Day Off* (1944), *Donald's Crime* (1945), *Canvas Back Duck* (1953), *Spare the Rod* (1954)

Writers:

Bill Berg, Al Bertino, David Detiege, Jack Kinney, Roy Williams, Ralph Wright

Director:

Jack Hannah

Broadcast:

Jan 15, 1958, ABC

Length:

53 min

The Saga of Andy Burnett: The Land of Enemies

Disneyland

Source:

The Saga of Andy Burnett #4

Writers:

Thomas W. Blackburn

Director:

Lewis R. Foster

Stars:

Jerome Courtland, Jeff York, Andrew Duggan, Slim Pickens

Broadcast:

Feb 26, 1958, ABC

Length:

53 min

The Saga of Andy Burnett: White Man's Medicine (1958)

Disneyland

Source:

The Saga of Andy Burnett #5

Writers:

Thomas W. Blackburn

Director:
Lewis R. Foster

Stars:
Jerome Courtland, Jeff York, Andrew Duggan, Slim Pickens

Broadcast:
Mar 5, 1958, ABC

Length:
53 min

The Saga of Andy Burnett: The Big Council (1958)

Disneyland

Source:
The Saga of Andy Burnett #6

Writers:
Thomas W. Blackburn

Director:
Lewis R. Foster

Stars:
Jerome Courtland, Jeff York, Andrew Duggan, Slim Pickens

Broadcast:
Mar 12, 1958, ABC

Length:
53 min

Magic and Music (1958)

Disneyland

Writers:
Milt Banta, Mary Blair, Otto Englander

Director:
Hamilton S. Luske

Broadcast:
Mar 19, 1958, ABC

Length:
52 min

Shorts:
Magic and Music (1974) Edited, educational

An Adventure in the Magic Kingdom (1958)

Disneyland

Source:
Behind the scenes of Disneyland

Writers:
Larry Clemmons

Director:
Hamilton S. Luske

Broadcast:
Apr 9, 1958, ABC

Length:
53 min

TV Serial:
An Adventure in the Magic Kingdom (1958-1959) Mickey Mouse club serialisation

Four Tales on a Mouse (1958)

Disneyland

Includes:
The Whalers (1938), *The Pointer* (1939), *The Little Whirlwind* (1941), *The Nifty Nineties* (1941), *Mickey's Birthday Party* (1942), *Pluto's Christmas Tree* (1952)

Writers:
Bill Berg, Nick George

Director:
Hamilton S. Luske

Broadcast:
Apr 16, 1958, ABC

Length:
53 min

An Adventure in Art (1958)

Disneyland

Source:
The Art Spirit (1923) Robert Henri

Writers:
Lee Blair, Dick Huemer

Directors:
Wilfred Jackson, C. August Nichols

Broadcast:
Apr 30, 1958, ABC

Length:
53 min

Shorts:
4 Artists Paint 1 Tree (1964) Educational, excerpt

DVD*/Blu-ray:
2003 *Sleeping Beauty: Special Edition** (16 min excerpt), 2008 *Sleeping Beauty: Platinum Edition* (16 min excerpt)

Magic Highway, U.S.A. (1958)

Disneyland

Writers:
Larry Clemmons, Chuck Downs, John W. Dunn

Director:
Ward Kimball

Broadcast:
May 14, 1958, ABC

Length:
53 min

The Nine Lives of Elfego Baca (1958)

Walt Disney Presents

Source:
Life of Elfego Baca

Writers:
Norman Foster

Director:
Norman Foster

Stars:
Robert Loggia, Robert F. Simon, Lisa Montell, Nestor Paiva

Broadcast:
Oct 3, 1958, ABC

Length:
52 min

Comic Strips:
The Nine Lives of Elfego Baca (Four Color #997, Jun/Aug 1959)

Movies:
The Nine Lives of Elfego Baca (1959, Europe) Edited from TV episodes

TV Anthology:
- *Four Down and Five Lives to Go* (1958)
- *Lawman or Gunman* (1958)
- *Law and Order, Incorporated* (1958)
- *Attorney at Law* (1959)
- *The Griswold Murder* (1959)
- *Move Along Mustangers* (1959)
- *Mustang Man, Mustang Maid* (1959)
- *Friendly Enemies at Law* (1960)
- *Gus Tomlin is Dead* (1960)

Video:
1986

DVD:
2005 *WD Treasures: Elfego Baca The Swamp Fox: Legendary Heroes*

Book:
The Disney Live-Action Productions/Walt Disney and Live Action (1994/2016) John G. West

The Pigeon That Worked a Miracle (1958)

Walt Disney Presents

Source:
The Pigeon That Worked a Miracle (?) Thomas Ligget

Writers:
Otto Englander

Director:
Walter Perkins

Stars:
Bradley Payne, Winifred Davenport

Broadcast:
Oct 10, 1958, ABC

Length:
52 min

Shorts:
1962, International

Four Down and Five Lives to Go (1958)

Walt Disney Presents

Source:
Elfego Baca #2

Writers:
Norman Foster

Director:
Norman Foster

Stars:
Robert Loggia, Robert F. Simon, Lisa Montell, Nestor Paiva

Broadcast:
Oct 17, 1958, ABC

Length:
52 min

Movies:
The Nine Lives of Elfego Baca (1959, Europe) Edited from TV episodes

Video:
1986 *The Nine Lives of Elfego Baca*

DVD:
2005 *WD Treasures: Elfego Baca The Swamp Fox: Legendary Heroes*

Rusty and the Falcon (1958)

Walt Disney Presents

Source:
"The White Falcon" (1955) Charlton Ogburn

Director:
N. Paul Kenworthy

Stars:
Jerome Courtland, Rudy Lee, Jay W. Lee

Broadcast:
Oct 24, 1958, ABC

Length:
52 min

Shorts:
1966, International

Texas John Slaughter (1958)

Walt Disney Presents

Source:
Life of Texas Ranger John Slaughter
Writers:
Frank D. Gilroy, Burt Styler, Albert E. Lewin
Director:
Harry Keller
Stars:
Tom Tryon, Robert Middleton, Norma Moore, Harry Carey Jr.
Broadcast:
Oct 31, 1958, ABC
Length:
52 min
Comic Strips:
Texas John Slaughter (Four Color #1181, Apr/Jun 1961)
Movies:
Texas John Slaughter (1960, Malaysia/Europe/Etc.) Edited from TV episodes
TV Anthology:
- *Ambush at Laredo* (1958)
- *Killers from Kansas* (1959)
- *Showdown at Sandoval* (1959)
- *The Man from Bitter Creek* (1959)
- *The Slaughter Trail* (1959)
- *The Robber Stallion* (1959)
- *Wild Horse Revenge* (1959)
- *Range War at Tombstone* (1959)
- *Desperado from Tombstone* (1960)
- *Apache Friendship* (1960)
- *Kentucky Gunslick* (1960)
- *Geronimo's Revenge* (1960)
- *End of the Trail* (1961)
- *A Holster Full of Law* (1961)
- *Trip to Tucson* (1961)
- *Frank Clell's in Town* (1961)

Book:
The Disney Live-Action Productions/Walt Disney and Live Action (1994/2016) John G. West

Ambush at Laredo (1958)

Walt Disney Presents

Source:
Texas John Slaughter #2

Writers:
Frank D. Gilroy, Burt Styler

Director:
Harry Keller

Stars:
Tom Tryon, Robert Middleton, Harry Carey Jr., Norma Moore

Broadcast:
Nov 14, 1958, ABC

Length:
52 min

Movies:
Texas John Slaughter (1960, Malaysia/Europe/Etc.) Edited from TV episodes

Lawman or Gunman (1958)

Walt Disney Presents

Source:
Elfego Baca #3

Director:
Christian Nyby

Stars:
Robert Loggia, James Dunn, Ramon Novarro, Skip Homeier

Broadcast:
Nov 28, 1958, ABC

Length:
52 min

Law and Order, Incorporated (1958)

Walt Disney Presents

Source:
Elfego Baca #4

Director:
Christian Nyby

Stars:
Robert Loggia, James Dunn, Ramon Novarro, Skip Homeier

Broadcast:
Dec 12, 1958, ABC
Length:
52 min

From All of Us, to All of You (1958)

Walt Disney Presents
Includes:
Santa's Workshop (1932), *Toy Tinkers* (1949)
Writers:
Al Bertino, David Detiege
Director:
Jack Hannah
Broadcast:
Dec 19, 1958, ABC
Length:
52 min
TV Anthology:
- 1963, 1967, 1970, 1973, 1977, 1979, 1980 (Updated versions)
- *A Disney Channel Christmas* (1983) Extended Disney Channel version

Video/Laserdisc:
1986 *Jiminy Cricket's Christmas*
Books:
The Vault of Walt: Volume 7—Christmas Edition (2018) Jim Korkis

Killers from Kansas (1959)

Walt Disney Presents
Source:
Texas John Slaughter #3
Writers:
Frank D. Gilroy
Director:
Harry Keller
Stars:
Tom Tryon, Lyle Bettger, Beverly Garland, Norma Moore
Broadcast:
Jan 9, 1959, ABC

Length:
52 min
Movies:
Gunfight at Sandoval (1960, International) Edited from TV episodes

Showdown at Sandoval (1959)

Walt Disney Presents
Source:
Texas John Slaughter #4
Writers:
Frank D. Gilroy, Maurice Tombragel
Director:
Harry Keller
Stars:
Tom Tryon, Dan Duryea, Beverly Garland, Norma Moore
Broadcast:
Jan 23, 1959, ABC
Length:
52 min
Movies:
Gunfight at Sandoval (1960, International) Edited from TV episodes

The Peter Tchaikovsky Story (1959)

Walt Disney Presents
Source:
Life of Peter Tchaikovsky
Writers:
Otto Englander, Joe Rinaldi
Director:
Charles Barton
Stars:
Grant Williams, Rex Hill, Lilyan Chauvin, Leon Askin
Broadcast:
Jan 30, 1959, ABC
Length:
49 min
Shorts:
1959, International

DVD*/Blu-ray:
2003 *Sleeping Beauty: Special Edition** (30 min excerpt), 2008 *Sleeping Beauty: Platinum Edition*

Attorney at Law (1959)

Walt Disney Presents

Source:
Elfego Baca #5

Writers:
Maurice Tombragel

Director:
Christian Nyby

Stars:
Robert Loggia, James Dunn, Lynn Bari, Kenneth Tobey

Broadcast:
Feb 6, 1959

Length:
52 min

Movies:
Six Gun Law (1962, UK) Edited from TV episodes

Video:
1986 *Six Gun Law*

DVD:
2005 *WD Treasures: Elfego Baca The Swamp Fox: Legendary Heroes*

Duck Flies Coop (1959)

Walt Disney Presents

Includes:
Chip an' Dale (1947), *Winter Storage* (1949), *Trailer Horn* (1950), *Rugged Bear* (1953), *Grin and Bear It* (1954), *Bearly Asleep* (1955)

Writers:
Al Bertino, David Detiege

Director:
Jack Hannah

Broadcast:
Feb 13, 1959, ABC

Length:
52 min

TV Special:
Down and Out with Donald Duck (1987) Edited from episode

The Griswold Murder (1959)

Walt Disney Presents

Source:
Elfego Baca #6

Writers:
Maurice Tombragel

Director:
Christian Nyby

Stars:
Robert Loggia, James Dunn, Jay C. Flippen, Patrick Knowles

Broadcast:
Feb 20, 1959, ABC

Length:
52 min

Movies:
Six Gun Law (1962, UK) Edited from TV episodes

Video:
1986 *Six Gun Law*

The Adventures of Chip 'n' Dale (1959)

Walt Disney Presents

AKA:
Mixed Nuts (1978), *The Misadventures of Chip 'n' Dale* (1980+)

Includes:
Chicken in the Rough (1951), *Donald Applecore* (1952), *Two Chips and a Miss* (1952), *The Lone Chipmunks* (1954), *Up a Tree* (1955), *Chips Ahoy* (1956)

Writers:
Bill Berg, Nick George, Dick Kinney, Milt Schaffer

Director:
Bill Justice

Broadcast:
Feb 27, 1959, ABC

Length:
52 min

DiscoVision:
1979
Video:
Unknown

The Man from Bitter Creek (1959)
Walt Disney Presents
Source:
Texas John Slaughter #5
Director:
Harry Keller
Stars:
Tom Tryon, Stephen McNally, Sidney Blackmer, Bill Williams
Broadcast:
Mar 6, 1959
Length:
52 min
Movies:
Stampede at Bitter Creek (1962, International) Edited from TV episodes
[Collection: Video, 1986]

Highway to Trouble (1959)
Walt Disney Presents
Includes:
Sea Scouts (1939), *Grand Canyonscope* (1954), *The Hockey Champ* (1939),
Donald's Camera (1941)
Writers:
Al Bertino, David Detiege, Nick George
Director:
Jack Hannah
Broadcast:
Mar 13, 1959, ABC
Length:
52 min

The Slaughter Trail (1959)
Walt Disney Presents
Source:
Texas John Slaughter #6

Director:
Harry Keller

Stars:
Tom Tryon, Sidney Blackmer, Bill Williams, John Larch

Broadcast:
Mar 20, 1959, ABC

Length:
52 min

Movies:
Stampede at Bitter Creek (1962, International) Edited from TV episodes [Collection: Video, 1986]

Toot, Whistle, Plunk and Boom (1959)

Walt Disney Presents

Includes:
Toot, Whistle, Plunk and Boom (1953), *Music Land* (1935), *Melody* (1953), *Jack and Old Mac* (1956), *A Cowboy Needs a Horse* (1956)

Director:
Wilfred Jackson

Broadcast:
Mar 27, 1959, ABC

Length:
52 min

I Captured the King of the Leprechauns (1959)

Walt Disney Presents

Source:
Behind the scenes of *Darby O'Gill and the Little People* (1959)

Writers:
Lawrence Edward Watkin

Director:
Harry Keller

Broadcast:
May 29, 1959, ABC

Length:
49 min

DVD:
2004 *Darby O'Gill and the Little People,* 2006 *WD Treasures: Your Host, Walt Disney,* 2012 *Disney 4-Movie Collection: Classics*

Digital:
Amazon

Disneyland '59 (1959)

Sponsored by Kodak

AKA:
Kodak Presents Disneyland '59

Source:
5th, anniversary of Disneyland

Writers:
Larry Clemmons

Directors:
Marshall Diskin, Hamilton S. Luske

Broadcast:
Jun 15, 1959, ABC

Length:
89 min

DVD:
2006 WD Treasures: Your Host, Walt Disney

Moochie of the Little League (1959)

Walt Disney Presents

AKA:
Little League Moochie (16 mm)

Episodes:
A Diamond is a Boy's Best Friend (Part 1) & *Wrong Way Moochie* (Part 2)

Writers:
Ellis Marcus

Director:
William Beaudine

Stars:
Kevin Corcoran, Reginald Owen, Alan Hale Jr., Stuart Erwin

Broadcast:
Oct 2, 1959 (Part 1), Oct 9, 1959 (Part 2), ABC

Length:
94 min

TV Anthology:
Moochie of Pop Warner Football (1960) Sequel

TV Serial:
1960 (Serialized on *The Mickey Mouse Club*)

Killers of the High Country (1959)

Walt Disney Presents

Writers:
Lloyd Beebe, Arnold Belgard, Rutherford Montgomery, Donn Hale Munson

Director:
Tom McGowan

Broadcast:
Oct 16, 1959, ABC

Length:
52 min

The Birth of the Swamp Fox (1959)

Walt Disney Presents

Source:
Life of Francis Marion; *Swamp Fox* (1959) Robert D. Bass

Writers:
Lewis R. Foster

Director:
Harry Keller

Stars:
Leslie Nielsen, Joy Page, Tim Considine, John Sutton

Broadcast:
Oct 23, 1959, ABC

Length:
52 min

Comic Strips:
The Swamp Fox (Four Color #1179, Mar/May 1961)

TV Anthology:
- *Brother Against Brother* (1959)
- *Tory Vengeance* (1960)
- *Day of Reckoning* (1960)
- *Redcoat Strategy* (1960)
- *A Case of Treason* (1960)
- *A Woman's Courage* (1961)
- *Horses for Greene* (1961)

DVD:
2005 *WD Treasures: Elfego Baca The Swamp Fox: Legendary Heroes*
Book:
The Disney Live-Action Productions/Walt Disney and Live Action (1994/2016) John G. West

Brother Against Brother (1959)

Walt Disney Presents

Source:
The Swamp Fox #2

Writers:
Lewis R. Foster

Director:
Harry Keller

Stars:
Leslie Nielsen, Joy Page, John Sutton, Dick Foran

Broadcast:
Oct 30, 1959, ABC

Length:
52 min

DVD:
2005 *WD Treasures: Elfego Baca The Swamp Fox: Legendary Heroes*

Perilous Assignment (1959)

Walt Disney Presents

Source:
Behind the scenes of *Third Man on the Mountain* (1959)

Writers:
Dwight Hauser

Director:
Hamilton S. Luske

Broadcast:
Nov 6, 1959, ABC

Length:
48 min

Digital:
Amazon

Move Along, Mustangers (1959)

Walt Disney Presents

Source:
Elfego Baca #7

Director:
George Sherman

Stars:
Robert Loggia, Brian Keith, Arthur Hunnicutt, Beverly Garland

Broadcast:
Nov 13, 1959, ABC

Length:
52 min

Mustang Man, Mustang Maid (1959)

Walt Disney Presents

Source:
Elfego Baca #8

Director:
George Sherman

Stars:
Robert Loggia, Brian Keith, Arthur Hunnicutt, Beverly Garland

Broadcast:
Nov 20, 1959, ABC

Length:
52 min

A Storm Called Maria (1959)

Walt Disney Presents

Source:
Storm (1941) George R. Stewart

Director:
Ken Nelson

Broadcast:
Nov 27, 1959, ABC

Length:
52 min

The Robber Stallion (1959)

Walt Disney Presents

Source:
Texas John Slaughter #7

Writers:
Fred Freibeger

Director:
Harry Keller

Stars:
Tom Tryon, Darryl Hickman, Barton MacLane, John Vivyan

Broadcast:
Dec 4, 1959, ABC

Length:
52 min

Wild Horse Revenge (1959)

Walt Disney Presents

Source:
Texas John Slaughter #7A

Writers:
Fred Freiberger

Director:
Harry Keller

Stars:
Tom Tryon, Darryl Hickman, Barton MacLane, John Vivyan

Broadcast:
Dec 11, 1959, ABC

Length:
52 min

Range War at Tombstone (1959)

Walt Disney Presents

Source:
Texas John Slaughter #8

Writers:
David P. Harmon

Director:
Harry Keller

Stars:

Tom Tryon, Darryl Hickman, Betty Lynn, Regis Toomey

Broadcast:

Dec 18, 1959, ABC

Length:

52 min

PART TWO

1960–1964

Tory Vengeance (1960)

Walt Disney Presents

Source:
The Swamp Fox #3

Writers:
Lewis R. Foster

Director:
Louis King

Stars:
Leslie Nielsen, John Sutton, Henry Daniell, Barbara Eiler

Broadcast:
Jan 1, 1960, ABC

Length:
52 min

DVD:
2005 *WD Treasures: Elfego Baca The Swamp Fox: Legendary Heroes*

Day of Reckoning (1960)

Walt Disney Presents

Source:
The Swamp Fox #4

Writers:
Lewis R. Foster

Director:
Louis King

Stars:
Leslie Nielsen, John Sutton, Henry Daniell, Barbara Eiler

Broadcast:
Jan 8, 1960, ABC

Length:
52 min

Redcoat Strategy (1960)

Walt Disney Presents

Source:
The Swamp Fox #5

Writers:
Lewis R. Foster

Director:
Louis King

Stars:
Leslie Nielsen, Robert Douglas, John Sutton, Barbara Eiler

Broadcast:
Jan 15, 1960, ABC

Length:
52 min

A Case of Treason (1960)

Walt Disney Presents

Source:
The Swamp Fox #6

Writers:
Lewis R. Foster

Director:
Louis King

Stars:
Leslie Nielsen, Robert Douglas, Barbara Eiler, John Sutton

Broadcast:
Jan 22, 1960, ABC

Length:
52 min

Wild Burro of the West (1960)

Walt Disney Presents

Source:
Dusty's Return (1950) Dorothy Childs Hogner

Director:
Walter Perkins

Stars:
Bill Keys, Bill Pace, Jim Burch

Broadcast:
Jan 29, 1960, ABC

Length:
52 min

Two Happy Amigos (1960)

Walt Disney Presents

Includes:
Aquarela do Brasil (1942), *Honey Harvester* (1949), *Morris the Midget Moose* (1950)

Directors:
Jack Hannah, C. August Nichols

Broadcast:
Feb 5, 1960, ABC

Length:
52 min

Desperado from Tombstone (1960)

Walt Disney Presents

Source:
Texas John Slaughter #9

Writers:
Maurice Tombragel

Director:
Harry Keller

Stars:
Tom Tryon, Gene Evans, Regis Toomey, Betty Lynn

Broadcast:
Feb 12, 1950, ABC

Length:
52 min

Apache Friendship (1960)

Walt Disney Presents

Source:
Texas John Slaughter #10

Writers:
Maurice Tombragel

Director:
Harry Keller

Stars:
Tom Tryon, Gene Evans, Regis Toomey, Betty Lynn

Broadcast:
Feb 19, 1960, ABC

Length:
52 min

Kentucky Gunslick (1960)

Walt Disney Presents

Source:
Texas John Slaughter #11

Writers:
David P. Harmon

Director:
Harry Keller

Stars:
Tom Tryon, Darryl Hickman, Betty Lynn, Brian Corcoran

Broadcast:
Feb 26, 1960, ABC

Length:
52 min

Geronimo's Revenge (1960)

Walt Disney Presents

Source:
Texas John Slaughter #12

Writers:
David P. Harmon

Director:
Harry Keller

Stars:
Tom Tryon, Darryl Hickman, Betty Lynn, Brian Corcoran

Broadcast:
Mar 4, 1960, ABC

Length:
52 min
Movies:
Geronimo's Revenge (1964, Europe) Edited from TV episodes [Collection: Video, 1986]

This is Your Life, Donald Duck (1960)
Walt Disney Presents
Source:
Various Donald Duck shorts (1937-1954)
Writers:
Al Bertino, David Detiege, Nick George
Directors:
Jack Hannah, C. August Nichols
Broadcast:
Mar 11, 1960, ABC
Length:
52 min
Comic Strips:
This Is Your Life Donald Duck (Four Color #1109, Aug/Oct 1960)

Friendly Enemies at Law (1960)
Walt Disney Presents
Source:
Elfego Baca #9
Writers:
Barney Slater
Director:
William Beaudine
Stars:
Robert Loggia, John Kerr, Patricia Crowley, Barton MacLane
Broadcast:
Mar 18, 1960, ABC
Length:
52 min

Gus Tomlin is Dead (1960)

Walt Disney Presents

Source:
Elfego Baca #10

Writers:
Fred Freiberger

Director:
William Beaudine

Stars:
Robert Loggia, Alan Hale Jr., Coleen Gray, Brian Corcoran

Broadcast:
Mar 25, 1960, ABC

Length:
52 min

The Mad Hermit of Chimney Butte (1960)

Walt Disney Presents

Source:
Various Donald Duck shorts

Director:
Jack Hannah

Broadcast:
Apr 1, 1960, ABC

Length:
52 min

Rapids Ahead (1960)

Walt Disney Presents (½ episode)

Includes:
Bear Country (1953)

Source:
Behind the scenes of *Ten Who Dared* (1960)

Director:
William Beaudine

Broadcast:
Oct 16, 1960, ABC

Length:
20 min

El Bandido (1960)

Walt Disney Presents

Source:
Sequel to *Zorro* (1957-1959) TV series

Writers:
Bob Wehling

Director:
William Witney

Stars:
Guy Williams, Henry Calvin, Gene Sheldon, Rita Moreno

Broadcast:
Oct 30, 1960, ABC

Length:
51 min

TV Anthology:
- *Adios El Cuchillo* (1960)
- *The Postponed Wedding* (1961)
- *Auld Aquaintance* (1961)

DVD:
2009 *WD Treasures: Zorro: The Complete First Season*

Adios El Cuchillo (1960)

Walt Disney Presents

Source:
Sequel to *El Bandido* (1960)

Writers:
Bob Wehling

Director:
William Witney

Stars:
Guy Williams, Henry Calvin, Gene Sheldon, Rita Moreno

Broadcast:
Nov 6, 1960, ABC

Length:
51 min

DVD:
2009 *WD Treasures: Zorro: The Complete First Season*

Donald's Silver Anniversary (1960)

Walt Disney Presents

Source:
Various Donald Duck shorts

Writers:
Bill Berg, Larry Clemmons

Director:
Hamilton S. Luske

Broadcast:
Nov 13, 1960, ABC

Length:
52 min

Moochie of Pop Warner Football (1960)

Walt Disney Presents

Episodes:
Pee Wees Versus City Hall (Part 1) & *From Ticonderoga to Disneyland* (Part 2)

Source:
Sequel to *Moochie of the Little League* (1959)

Director:
William Beaudine

Stars:
Kevin Corcoran, Dennis Joel, Reginald Owen, John Howard

Broadcast:
Nov 20, 1960 (Part 1) & Nov 27, 1960 (Part 2), ABC

Length:
90 min

TV Serial:
1960s (Serialized on *The Mickey Mouse Club*)

The Warrior's Path (1960)

Walt Disney Presents

Source:
Life of Daniel Boone

Writers:
David Victor

Director:
Lewis R. Foster

Stars:
Dewey Martin, Mala Powers, Richard Banke, Eddy Waller

Broadcast:
Dec 4, 1960, ABC

Length:
52 min

TV Anthology:
- *And Chase the Buffalo* (1960)
- *The Wilderness Road* (1961)
- *The Promised Land* (1961)

Book:
The Disney Live-Action Productions/Walt Disney and Live Action (1994/2016) John G. West

And Chase the Buffalo (1960)

Walt Disney Presents

Source:
Daniel Boone #2

Writers:
David Victor

Director:
Lewis R. Foster

Stars:
Dewey Martin, Mala Powers, Kevin Corcoran, Brian Corcoran

Broadcast:
Dec 11, 1960, ABC

Length:
52 min

Escape to Paradise (1960)

Walt Disney Presents (½ episode)

Includes:
Water Birds (1952)

Source:
Behind the scenes of *Swiss Family Robinson* (1960)

Writers:
Larry Clemmons

Broadcast:
Dec 18, 1960, ABC

Length:
23 min
DVD:
2002 *Swiss Family Robinson: Vault Disney Collection*

The Postponed Wedding (1961)

Walt Disney Presents

Source:
Sequel to *Zorro* (1957-1959) TV series
Writers:
Roy Edward Disney, Bob Wehling
Director:
James Neilson
Stars:
Guy Williams, Annette Funicello, Henry Calvin, Gene Sheldon
Broadcast:
Jan 1, 1961, ABC
Length:
52 min
DVD:
2009 *WD Treasures: Zorro: The Complete Second Season*

A Woman's Courage (1961)

Walt Disney Presents

Source:
The Swamp Fox #7
Director:
Lewis R. Foster
Stars:
Leslie Nielsen, Barbara Eiler, Arthur Hunnicutt, Sean McClory
Broadcast:
Jan 8, 1961, ABC
Length:
52 min

Horses for Greene (1961)

Walt Disney Presents

Source:
The Swamp Fox #8

Director:
Lewis R. Foster

Stars:
Leslie Nielsen, Barbara Eiler, Arthur Hunnicutt, Ralph Clanton

Broadcast:
Jan 15, 1961, ABC

Length:
52 min

A Salute to Father (1961)

Walt Disney Presents

AKA:
Goofy's Salute to Father

Source:
Various Goofy shorts (1950-1953)

Writers:
Otto Englander, Joe Rinaldi

Director:
Wolfgang Reitherman

Broadcast:
Jan 22, 1961, ABC

Length:
52 min

Laserdisc:
1981 *Disney Cartoon Parade: Vol 3*

End of the Trail (1961)

Walt Disney Presents

Source:
Texas John Slaughter #13

Director:
James Neilson

Stars:
Tom Tryon, Betty Lynn, Onslow Stevens, Harry Carey Jr.

Broadcast:
Jan 29, 1961, ABC

Length:
52 min

Movies:
Geronimo's Revenge (1964, Europe) Edited from TV episodes [Collection: Video, 1986]

A Holster Full of Law (1961)

Walt Disney Presents

Source:
Texas John Slaughter #14

Director:
James Neilson

Stars:
Tom Tryon, Betty Lynn, R.G. Armstrong, Jim Beck

Broadcast:
Feb 5, 1961, ABC

Length:
52 min

Movies:
A Holster Full of Law (1966, Europe) Edited from TV episodes

The Coyote's Lament (1961)

Walt Disney Presents

Source:
Various shorts (1939-1951)

Writers:
Eric Gurney, Dick Kinney, Lance Nolley, Milt Schaffer

Director:
C. August Nichols

Broadcast:
Mar 5, 1961, ABC

Length:
52 min

Shorts:
The Coyote's Lament (1968, Europe)

TV Movie:
Coyote Tails (1991) Extended remake

DiscoVision:
1979

The Wilderness Road (1961)

Walt Disney Presents

Source:
Daniel Boone #3

Director:
Lewis R. Foster

Stars:
Dewey Martin, Mala Powers, Diane Jergens, William Herrin

Broadcast:
Mar 12, 1961, ABC

Length:
52 min

The Promised Land (1961)

Walt Disney Presents

Source:
Daniel Boone #4

Director:
Lewis R. Foster

Stars:
Dewey Martin, Mala Powers, Diane Jergens, William Herrin

Broadcast:
Mar 19, 1961, ABC

Length:
52 min

Auld Acquaintance (1961)

Walt Disney Presents

Source:
Sequel to *Zorro* (1957-1959) TV series

Writers:
Bob Wehling

Director:
James Neilson

Stars:
Guy Williams, Henry Calvin, Gene Sheldon, Ricardo Montalban

Broadcast:
Apr 2, 1961, ABC

Length:
52 min

DVD:
2009 *WD Treasures: Zorro: The Complete Second Season*

Battle for Survival (1961)

Walt Disney Presents

Director:
James Algar

Broadcast:
Apr 9, 1961, ABC

Length:
52 min

Trip to Tucson (1961)

Walt Disney Presents

Source:
Texas John Slaughter #15

Writers:
Maurice Tombragel

Director:
James Neilson

Stars:
Tom Tryon, Betty Lynn, Joe Maross, Jim Beck

Broadcast:
Apr 16, 1961, ABC

Length:
52 min

Movies:
A Holster Full of Law (1966, Europe) Edited from TV episodes

Frank Clell's in Town (1961)

Walt Disney Presents

Source:
Texas John Slaughter #16

Writers:
Maurice Tombragel

Director:
James Neilson

Stars:
Tom Tryon, Betty Lynn, Brian Corcoran, Jim Beck

Broadcast:
Apr 23, 1961, ABC

Length:
52 min

Movies:
A Holster Full of Law (1966, Europe) Edited from TV episodes

Flash, the Teenage Otter (1961)

Walt Disney Presents

AKA:
Flash, the Teen-Age Otter

Director:
Hank Schloss

Broadcast:
Apr 30, 1961, ABC

Length:
52 min

Shorts:
1964 (Europe), 1965 (US)

Video:
?? *The Yellowstone Cubs*

Wonders of the Water World (1961)

Walt Disney Presents

Source:
True-Life Adventures series

Writers:
Roy Edward Disney

Director:
Winston Hibler

Broadcast:
May 21, 1961, ABC

Length:
50 min

DVD:
2006 *WD Legacy Collection: True-Life Adventures Vol 1—Wonders of the World*

Books:
True-Life Adventures: A History of Walt Disney's Nature Documentaries (2017) Christian Moran

The Titlemakers (1961)

Walt Disney Presents (½ episode)

Includes:
Nature's Half Acre (1951)

Source:
Behind the scenes of *The Parent Trap* (1961)

Director:
Robert Stevenson

Broadcast:
Jun 11, 1961, ABC

Length:
17 min

DVD:
2002 *The Parent Trap: Vault Disney Collection,* 2005 *The Parent Trap: 2-Movie Collection*

Books:
True-Life Adventures: A History of Walt Disney's Nature Documentaries (2017) Christian Moran

An Adventure in Color (1961)

Walt Disney's Wonderful World of Color (½ episode)

Includes:
Donald in Mathmagic Land (1959)

Writers:
Larry Clemmons, Otto Englander, Joe Rinaldi

Director:
Hamilton S. Luske

Broadcast:
Sep 24, 1961, NBC

Length:
22 min

Video:
1986 *The Wonderful World of Disney: An Adventure in Color including Donald in Mathmagic Land*

Digital:
Vudu (as *An Adventure in Color—Mathmagic Land,* 50 min)

The Horsemasters (1961)
Walt Disney's Wonderful World of Color
Episodes:
Follow Your Heart (Part 1), & *Tally Ho* (Part 2)
Source:
The Horsemasters (1957) Don Stanford
Writers:
William Fairchild, Ted Willis
Director:
William Fairchild
Stars:
Annette Funicello, Tommy Kirk, Janet Fraser, Donald Pleasance
Broadcast:
Oct 1, 1961 (Part 1), Oct 8, 1961 (Part 2), NBC
Length:
85 min
Comic Strips:
The Horsemasters (Four Color #1260, Dec 1961/Feb 1962)
Movies:
1961 (Europe)
Video:
1986
Book:
The Disney Live-Action Productions/Walt Disney and Live Action (1994/2016) John G. West

Chico, the Misunderstood Coyote (1961)
Walt Disney's Wonderful World of Color
Writers:
Ernest Thompson Seton
Director:
Walter Perkins
Broadcast:
Oct 15, 1961, NBC
Length:
52 min

Shorts:
1962 (International)

The Hunting Instinct (1961)
Walt Disney's Wonderful World of Color

Source:
Various shorts (1938-1955)

Writers:
Bill Berg, Ted Berman, Otto Englander, Joe Rinaldi

Director:
Wolfgang Reitherman

Broadcast:
Oct 22, 1961, NBC

Length:
52 min

Shorts:
1962 (France), 1963 (Italy/Mexico/Finland), 1965 (Japan)

TV Anthology:
Man's Hunting Instinct (1982) Edited from this episode

Inside Donald Duck (1961)
Walt Disney's Wonderful World of Color

Source:
Various Donald Duck shorts (1940-1954)

Writers:
Bill Berg, Larry Clemmons, Roy Williams

Director:
Hamilton S. Luske

Broadcast:
Nov 5, 1961, NBC

Length:
52 min

Holiday for Henpecked Husbands (1961)
Walt Disney's Wonderful World of Color

AKA:
Goofy Takes a Holiday

Source:
Various Goofy shorts (1942-1953)

Writers:
Eric Cleworth, Lancy Nolley, Bill Peet

Director:
Wolfgang Reitherman

Broadcast:
Nov 26, 1961, NBC

Length:
52 min

A Fire Called Jeremiah (1961)

Walt Disney's Wonderful World of Color

Writers:
Dwight Hauser

Director:
James Algar

Broadcast:
Dec 3, 1961, NBC

Length:
52 min

Shorts:
1962 (International)

Kids is Kids (1961)

Walt Disney's Wonderful World of Color

AKA:
Donald Duck Quacks Up

Source:
Good Scouts (1938), *The Hockey Champ* (1939), *Soup's On* (1948), *Donald's Happy Birthday* (1949), *Lucky Number* (1951), *Don's Fountain of Youth* (1953)

Writers:
Bill Berg

Director:
Hamilton S. Luske

Broadcast:
Dec 10, 1961, NBC

Length:
48 min

Shorts:
1965 (International)

TV Anthology:
Mickey and Donald Kidding Around (1983) Edited version

DiscoVision:
1979

Laserdisc:
1981 *Disney Cartoon Parade: Vol 3*

Video:
1980

Backstage Party (1961)

Walt Disney's Wonderful World of Color

Source:
Behind the scenes of *Babes in Toyland* (1961)

Writers:
Larry Clemmons

Director:
Jack Donohue

Broadcast:
Dec 17, 1961, NBC

Length:
52 min

DVD:
2006 *WD Treasures: Your Host, Walt Disney*

Hans Brinker, or the Silver Skates (1962)

Walt Disney's Wonderful World of Color

Source:
The Silver Skates (1865) Mary Mapes Dodge

Writers:
Norman Foster

Director:
Norman Foster

Stars:
Rony Zeander, Carin Rossby, Gunilla Jelf, Erik Strandmark

Broadcast:
Jan 7, 1962 (Part 1), Jan 14, 1962 (Part 2), NBC

Length:
90 min
Comic Strips:
Hans Brinker (Four Color #1273, Mar/May 1962)
Movies:
1964 (International)
DVD:
2004

Sancho, the Homing Steer (1962)

Walt Disney's Wonderful World of Color
Episodes:
Sancho on the Rancho... and Elsewhere (Part 1), *The Perils of a Homesick Steer* (Part 2)
Director:
Tom McGowan
Stars:
Bill Shurley, Rosita Fernandez, Arthur Curtis
Broadcast:
Jan 21, 1962, NBC (Part 1) & Jan 28, 1962, NBC (Part 2)
Length:
85 min
Movies:
1964 (International)

Fantasy on Skis (1962)

Walt Disney's Wonderful World of Color
Writers:
Larry Clemmons (screenplay), Fred Iselin (story)
Director:
Fred Iselin
Stars:
Susie Wirth
Broadcast:
Feb 4, 1962, NBC
Length:
52 min (Original), 28 min (Theatrical)
Shorts:
1975 (Theatrical)

Carnival Time (1962)

Walt Disney's Wonderful World of Color

Writers:
Bill Berg, Joe Rinaldi

Director:
Hamilton S. Luske

Broadcast:
Mar 4, 1962, NBC

Length:
52 min

Soundtrack:
1962 *Carnival Time featuring Professor Ludwig von Drake* (LP)

The Prince and the Pauper (1962)

Walt Disney's Wonderful World of Color

Episodes:
The Pauper King (Part 1), *The Merciful Law of the King* (Part 2), & *Long Live the Rightful King* (Part 3)

Source:
The Prince and the Pauper (1881) Mark Twain

Writers:
Jack Whittingham

Director:
Don Chaffey

Stars:
Guy Williams, Sean Scully, Laurence Naismith, Donald Houston

Broadcast:
Mar 11, 1962 (Part 1), Mar 18, 1962 (Part 2), Mar 25, 1962 (Part 3), NBC

Length:
93 min (feature), 3 x 50 min (episodes)

Comic Book:
The Prince and the Pauper (May/Jul 1962)

Movies:
1962 (International)

Shorts:
The Prince and the Pauper (1990) Based on same story

Video:
1982, 1984

Digital:
Amazon, iTunes, Vudu
Soundtrack:
1972 (LP)

Spy in the Sky (1962)
Walt Disney's Wonderful World of Color
Includes:
Eye in Outer Space (1959)
Source:
Behind the scenes of *Moon Pilot* (1962)
Directors:
Harmon Jones, Ward Kimball
Broadcast:
Apr 1, 1962, NBC
Length:
52 min

Von Drake in Spain (1962)
Walt Disney's Wonderful World of Color
Writers:
Bill Berg, Joe Rinaldi
Director:
Norman Foster
Broadcast:
Apr 8, 1962, NBC
Length:
52 min
Shorts:
1965 (International)

Disneyland After Dark (1962)
Walt Disney's Wonderful World of Color
Source:
Behind the scenes of Disneyland
Writers:
Larry Clemmons
Directors:
Hamilton S. Luske, William Beaudine

Broadcast:
Apr 15, 1962, NBC

Length:
47 min

Shorts:
1962 (International), 1963 (US)

DVD:
2001 *WD Treasures: Disneyland USA*

The Golden Horseshoe Revue (1962)

Walt Disney's Wonderful World of Color

Source:
10,000th performance of the Golden Horseshoe Revue (Disneyland, 1955-1986)

Writers:
Larry Clemmons

Director:
Ron Miller

Broadcast:
Sep 23, 1962, NBC

Length:
49 min

Shorts:
1963 (International), 1964 (US)

DVD:
2007 *WD Treasures: Disneyland: Secrets, Stories & Magic*

Escapade in Florence (1962)

Walt Disney's Wonderful World of Color

Source:
The Golden Doors (1957) Edward Fenton

Writers:
Bob Wehling, Maurice Tombragel

Director:
Steve Previn

Stars:
Tommy Kirk, Annette Funicello, Nino Castelnuovo, Ivan Desny

Broadcast:
Sep 30, 1962 (Part 1), Oct 7, 1962 (Part 2), NBC

Length:
82 min

Comic Book:
Escapade In Florence (Jan 1963)

Movies:
1963 (International)

DVD:
2013 Disney Movie Club Exclusive

Soundtrack:
1962 (LP)

Book:
The Disney Live-Action Productions/Walt Disney and Live Action (1994/2016) John G. West

The Silver Fox and Sam Davenport (1962)
Walt Disney's Wonderful World of Color

Director:
Hank Schloss

Stars:
Gordon Perry

Broadcast:
Oct 14, 1962, NBC

Length:
52 min

Shorts:
1964 (International), 1972 (US)

Man is His Own Worst Enemy (1962)
Walt Disney's Wonderful World of Color

AKA:
Ducking Disaster with Donald and His Friends

Source:
Various shorts (1943-1960)

Writers:
Bill Berg, Joe Rinaldi

Director:
Hamilton S. Luske

Broadcast:
Oct 21, 1962, NBC

Length:
50 min

DVD:
1980s *Ducking Disaster with Donald and His Friends*

Sammy, the Way-Out Seal (1962)
Walt Disney Wonderful World of Color

Writers:
Norman Tokar

Director:
Norman Tokar

Stars:
Michael McGreevey, Billy Mumy, Jack Carson, Robert Culp

Broadcast:
Oct 28, 1962 (Part 1), Nov 4, 1962 (Part 2), NBC

Length:
89 min

Movies:
1963 (International)

Video:
1986

DVD:
2012 Disney Movie Club Exclusive

Digital:
Amazon, iTunes, Vudu

The Magnificent Rebel (1962)
Walt Disney's Wonderful World of Color

Source:
Life of Ludwig van Beethoven

Writers:
Joanne Court

Director:
Georg Tressler

Stars:
Karl Boehm, Giulia Rubini, Peter Arens, Ivan Desny

Broadcast:
Nov 18, 1962 (Part 1), Nov 25, 1962 (Part 2), NBC

Length:
101 min
Movies:
1961 (Europe)
DVD:
2012 Disney Movie Club Exclusive
Digital:
Amazon, iTunes, Vudu
Book:
The Disney Live-Action Productions/Walt Disney and Live Action (1994/2016) John G. West

The Mooncussers (1962)

Walt Disney's Wonderful World of Color

AKA:
Mooncussers
Episodes:
Graveyard of Ships (Part 1) & *Wake of Disaster* (Part 2)
Source:
Flying Ebony (1947) Iris Vinton
Writers:
Lowell S. Hawley
Director:
James Neilson
Stars:
Oscar Homolka, Kevin Corcoran, Robert Emhardt, Joan Freeman
Broadcast:
Dec 2, 1962 (Part 1), Dec 9, 1962 (Part 2), NBC
Length:
85 min
Comic Strips:
The Mooncussers (Walt Disney's World of Adventure #1, Apr 1963)
Movies:
1966 (International)
Video:
1986

Hurricane Hannah (1962)

Walt Disney's Wonderful World of Color

Broadcast:
Dec 16, 1962, NBC

Length:
52 min

Holiday Time at Disneyland (1962)

Walt Disney's Wonderful World of Color

Source:
Behind the scenes at Disneyland

Director:
Hamilton S. Luske

Broadcast:
Dec 23, 1962, NBC

Length:
52 min

Three Tall Tales (1963)

Walt Disney's Wonderful World of Color

Includes:
Casey Bats Again (1954), *Paul Bunyan* (1958), *The Saga of Windwagon Smith* (1961)

Writers:
Lance Nolley, Joe Rinaldi

Director:
Hamilton S. Luske

Broadcast:
Jan 6, 1963, NBC

Length:
52 min

Little Dog Lost (1963)

Walt Disney's Wonderful World of Color

Source:
Hurry Home, Candy (1953) Meindert de Jong

Writers:
Catherine Turney

Director:
Walter Perkins

Stars:
Hollis Black, Margaret Gerrity, Grace Bauer, Priscilla Overton

Broadcast:
Jan 13, 1963, NBC

Length:
49 min

DVD:
2008 Disney Movie Club Exclusive

Johnny Shiloh (1963)

Walt Disney's Wonderful World of Color

Source:
Johnny Shiloh; a novel of the Civil War (1959) James A. Rhodes & Dean Jauchius

Writers:
Ronald Alexander

Director:
James Neilson

Stars:
Kevin Corcoran, Brian Keith, Darryl Hickman, Skip Homeier

Broadcast:
Jan 20, 1963 (Part 1), Jan 27, 1963 (Part 2), NBC

Length:
90 min

Comic Strips:
Johnny Shiloh (Walt Disney's World of Adventure #2, Jul 1963)

Movies:
1965 (Japan)

Video:
1987

DVD:
2011 Disney Movie Club Exclusive

Book:
The Disney Live-Action Productions/Walt Disney and Live Action (1994/2016) John G. West

Greta, the Misfit Greyhound (1963)

Walt Disney's Wonderful World of Color

Director:
Larry Lansburgh

Stars:
Tacolo Chacartegui

Broadcast:
Feb 3, 1963, NBC

Length:
52 min

Shorts:
1966 (International)

Inside Outer Space (1963)

Walt Disney's Wonderful World of Color

Source:
Footage from *Mars and Beyond* (TV 1957), *Man in Space* (TV 1955), *Man and the Moon* (TV 1955)

Writers:
Bill Berg, William Bosche, John W. Dunn

Director:
Hamilton S. Luske

Broadcast:
Feb 10, 1963, NBC

Length:
52 min

Square Peg in a Round Hole (1963)

Walt Disney's Wonderful World of Color

AKA:
A Square Peg in a Round Hole, Goofing Around with Donald Duck

Includes:
How to Sleep (1953), *Beezy Bear* (1955), *In the Bag* (1956), *The Litterbug* (1961), *Aquamania* (1961)

Writers:
Ted Berman, Al Bertino, David Detiege, Otto Englander

Director:
Hamilton S. Luske

Broadcast:
Mar 3, 1963, NBC

Length:
52 min

Shorts:
1965 (International)

Video:
1980s *Ducking Disaster with Donald and His Friends*

The Horse Without a Head (1963)

Walt Disney's Wonderful World of Color

Episodes:
The 100,000,000 Franc Train Robbery (Part 1) & *The Key to the Cache* (Part 2)

Source:
A Hundred Million Francs (1955) Paul Berna

Writers:
T.E.B. Clarke

Director:
Don Chaffey

Stars:
Jean-Pierre Aumont, Hebert Lom, Leo McKern, Pamela Franklin

Broadcast:
Sep 29, 1963 (Part 1), Oct 6, 1963 (Part 2), NBC

Length:
89 min

Comic Strips:
The Horse Without a Head (Jan 1964)

Movies:
1963 (Europe)

Video:
1980s

DVD:
2006 Disney Movie Club Exclusive

Digital:
Amazon, iTunes, Vudu

Book:
The Disney Live-Action Productions/Walt Disney and Live Action (1994/2016) John G. West

Fly with Von Drake (1963)

Walt Disney's Wonderful World of Color

Director:
Hamilton S. Luske

Broadcast:
Oct 13, 1963, NBC

Length:
50 min

Video:
1980s *Music for Everybody*

The Wahoo Bobcat (1963)

Walt Disney's Wonderful World of Color

Director:
Hank Schloss

Stars:
Jock MacGregor, Bill Dunnagan, Lloyd Shelton

Broadcast:
Oct 20, 1963, NBC

Length:
52 min

Shorts:
1965 (International)

Video:
1980s *Ida, the Offbeat Eagle*

The Waltz King (1963)

Walt Disney's Wonderful World of Color

Source:
Life of Johann Strauss, Jr.

Writers:
Fritz Eckhardt (story), Maurice Tombragel (screenplay)

Director:
Steve Previn

Stars:
Kerwin Mathews, Senta Berger, Brian Aherne, Peter Kraus

Broadcast:
Oct 27, 1963 (Part 1), Nov 3, 1963 (Part 2), NBC

Length:
95 min
Movies:
1964 (International)
Video:
1980s
DVD:
2011 Generations Collection

The Truth About Mother Goose (1963)

Walt Disney's Wonderful World of Color
Source:
The Truth About Mother Goose (1957)
Writers:
Joe Rinaldi, Homer Brightman
Director:
Hamilton S. Luske
Broadcast:
Nov 17, 1963, NBC
Length:
52 min

The Ballad of Hector the Stowaway Dog (1964)

Walt Disney's Wonderful World of Color
AKA:
The Million Dollar Collar (Theatrical), *Hector, the Stowaway Pup*
Episodes:
Where the Heck is Hector? (Part 1) & *Who the Heck is Hector?* (Part 2)
Source:
Hector the Stowaway Dog (1958) Kenneth M. Dodson
Director:
Vincent McEveety
Stars:
Guy Stockwell, Craig Hill, Eric Pohlmann, Walter Gotell
Broadcast:
Jan 5, 1964 (Part 1), Jan 12, 1964 (Part 2), NBC
Length:
90 min

Mediterranean Cruise (1964)

Walt Disney's Wonderful World of Color

Source:
Switzerland (1955), *Portugal* (1957)

Director:
Hamilton S. Luske

Broadcast:
Jan 19, 1964, NBC

Length:
50 min

The Restless Sea (1964)

Bell System Science Series

Writers:
William Bosche

Director:
Les Clark

Broadcast:
Jan 24, 1964, NBC

Length:
57 min

Shorts:
1979 Educational, Edited

Bristle Face (1964)

Walt Disney's Wonderful World of Color

AKA:
Fox Hunter

Source:
Bristle Face (1962) Zachary Ball

Director:
Bob Sweeney

Stars:
Brian Keith, Philip Alford, Jeff Donnell, Wallace Ford

Broadcast:
Jan 26, 1964 (Part 1), Feb 2, 1964 (Part 2), NBC

Length:
90 min

The Scarecrow of Romney Marsh (1964)

Walt Disney's Wonderful World of Color

AKA:

Dr. Syn, Alias the Scarecrow

Source:

Doctor Syn: A Tale of the Romney Marsh (1915) William Buchanan, Russell Thorndike

Writers:

Robert Westerby

Director:

James Neilson

Stars:

Patrick McGoohan, George Cole, Tony Britton, Michael Hordern

Broadcast:

Feb 9, 1964 (Part 1), Feb 16, 1964 (Part 2), Feb 23, 1964 (Part 3), NBC

Length:

3 x 50 min (episodes), 98 min (UK movie edit), 75 min (US movie edit)

Comic Strips:

The Scarecrow of Romney Marsh (Apr 1964)

Movies:

The Scarecrow of Romney Marsh (1963, UK), (1975, US)

Video:

1986

DVD:

2008 *WD Treasures: Dr. Syn: The Scarecrow of Romney Marsh* (Episodes & UK movie edit)

Book:

The Disney Live-Action Productions/Walt Disney and Live Action (1994/2016) John G. West

The Legend of Two Gypsy Dogs (1964)

Walt Disney's Wonderful World of Color

Director:

Dr. Istvan Homoki-Nagy

Broadcast:

Mar 1, 1964, NBC

Length:

50 min

For the Love of Willadean (1964)

Walt Disney's Wonderful World of Color

Episodes:
A Taste of Melon (Part 1) & *Treasure in the Haunted House* (Part 2)

Writers:
Borden Deal (story), Arnold Peyser, Lois Peyser (screenplay)

Director:
Byron Paul

Stars:
Ed Wynn, Michael McGreevey, Billy Mumy, Roger Mobley

Broadcast:
Mar 8, 1964 (Part 1), Mar 15, 1964 (Part 2), NBC

Length:
90 min

Video:
1980s

Book:
The Disney Live-Action Productions/Walt Disney and Live Action (1994/2016) John G. West

In Shape with Von Drake (1964)

Walt Disney's Wonderful World of Color

Source:
Various shorts (1941-1949)

Writers:
Hamilton S. Luske

Director:
Bill Berg

Broadcast:
Mar 22, 1964, NBC

Length:
50 min

Disneyland Goes to the World's Fair (1964)

Walt Disney's Wonderful World of Color

Writers:
Charles Shows, Bill Berg

Director:
Hamilton S. Luske

Broadcast:
May 17, 1964, NBC

Length:
50 min

DVD:
2007 *WD Treasures: Disneyland: Secrets, Stories & Magic*

Soundtrack:
2009 *Walt Disney and the 1964 World's Fair* (CD)

A Rag, a Bone, a Box of Junk (1964)

Walt Disney's Wonderful World of Color

Includes:
Noah's Ark (1959), *A Symposium on Popular Songs* (1962)

Director:
Bill Justice

Broadcast:
Oct 11, 1964, NBC

Length:
50 min

The Tenderfoot (1964)

Walt Disney's Wonderful World of Color

Source:
Arizona in the 50s (1954) James H. Tevis

Writers:
Maurice Tombragel

Director:
Byron Paul

Stars:
Brian Keith, Brandon de Wilde, James Whitmore, Richard Long

Broadcast:
Oct 18, 1964 (Part 1), Oct 5, 1964 (Part 2), Nov 1, 1964 (Part 3), NBC

Length:
3 x 50 mins

Movies:
1966 (Europe)

One Day at Teton Marsh (1964)

Walt Disney's Wonderful World of Color

Source:

One Day at Teton Marsh (1965) Sally Carrighar

Broadcast:

Nov 8, 1964, NBC

Length:

50 min

Short:

1966 Educational, 16mm

PART THREE

1965–1969

Disneyland 10th Anniversary (1965)

Walt Disney's Wonderful World of Color

AKA:

The Disneyland Tenth Anniversary Show

Writer:

Bill Berg

Director:

Hamilton S. Luske

Broadcast:

Jan 3, 1965, NBC

Length:

46 min

DVD:

2001 WD Treasures: *Disneyland USA*, 2006 *WD Treasures: Your Host, Walt Disney*

Ida, the Offbeat Eagle (1965)

Walt Disney's Wonderful World of Color

Writers:

Homer McCoy, Jack Speirs (screenplay), Rutherford Montgomery (story)

Stars:

Clifton E. Carver

Broadcast:

Jan 10, 1965, NBC

Length:

48 min

Video:

1980s

Gallegher (1965)

Walt Disney's Wonderful World of Color

AKA:
The Adventures of Gallegher

Source:
Gallegher, and Other Stories (1891) Richard Harding Davis

Writers:
Maurice Tombragel

Director:
Byron Paul

Stars:
Roger Mobley, Edmond O'Brien, Jack Warden, Ray Teal

Broadcast:
Jan 24, 1965 (Part 1), Jan 31, 1965 (Part 2), Feb 7, 1965 (Part 3), NBC

Length:
3 x 50 mins

Comic Strips:
Gallegher, Boy Reporter (May 1965)

Movies:
1969 (International)

TV Anthology:
- *The Further Adventures of Gallegher* (1965) x 3 episodes
- *Gallegher Goes West* (1966-1967) x 4 episodes
- *The Mystery of Edward Sims* (1968) x 2 episodes

Book:
The Disney Live-Action Productions/Walt Disney and Live Action (1994/2016) John G. West

An Otter in the Family (1965)

Walt Disney's Wonderful World of Color

Stars:
Tom Beecham, Mable Beecham, Gary Beecham, Donald Cyr

Broadcast:
Feb 21, 1965, NBC

Length:
50 min

Kilroy (1965)

Walt Disney's Wonderful World of Color

Writers:
John Whedon (screenplay), Bart Burns, Betty Fernandez, Lee Pape (story)

Directors:
Robert Butler, Norman Tokar

Stars:
Warren Berlinger, Celeste Holm, Allyn Joslyn, Bryan Russell

Broadcast:
Mar 14, 1965 (Part 1), Mar 21, 1965 (Part 2), Mar 28, 1965 (Part 3), Apr 4, 1965 (Part 4), NBC

Length:
4 x 50 min

The Further Adventures of Gallegher (1965)

Walt Disney's Wonderful World of Color

Source:
Follows *Gallegher* (1965)

Episodes:
A Case of Murder (Part 1), *The Big Swindle* (Part 2), *The Daily Press vs. City Hall* (Part 3)

Writers:
Maurice Tombragel

Director:
Jeffrey Hayden

Stars:
Roger Mobley, Edmond O'Brien, Harvey Korman, Anne Francis

Broadcast:
Sep 26, 1965 (Part 1), Oct 3, 1965 (Part 2), Oct 10, 1965 (Part 3), NBC

Length:
3 x 50 min

Minado, the Wolverine (1965)

Walt Disney's Wonderful World of Color

Broadcast:
Nov 7, 1965, NBC

Length:
50 min

Shorts:
1978 (International)

Music for Everybody (1966)

Walt Disney's Wonderful World of Color

Source:
Various shorts and films (1946-1962)

Writers:
Joe Rinaldi

Director:
Hamilton S. Luske

Broadcast:
Jan 30, 1966, NBC

Length:
50 min

Video:
1980s

The Legend of Young Dick Turpin (1966)

Walt Disney's Wonderful World of Color

Source:
Life of Dick Turpin (1705-1739)

Writers:
Robert Westerby

Director:
James Neilson

Stars:
David Weston, Bernard Lee, George Cole, Maurice Denham

Broadcast:
Feb 13, 1966 (Part 1), Feb 20, 1966 (Part 2), NBC

Length:
89 min

Comic Book:
The Legend of Young Dick Turpin (May 1966)

Movies:
1965 (International)

Video:
1980s (UK)

Book:
The Disney Live-Action Productions/Walt Disney and Live Action (1994/2016) John G. West

Ballerina (1966)

Walt Disney's Wonderful World of Color

AKA:
Ballerina: A Story of the Royal Danish Ballet

Writers:
Casey Robinson, Robert Westerby (screenplay), Peter Schnitzler (story)

Director:
Norman Campbell

Stars:
Kirsten Simone, Astrid Villaume, Ole Wegener, Poul Reichardt

Broadcast:
Feb 27, 1966 (Part 1), Mar 6, 1966 (Part 2), NBC

Length:
2 x 50 min

Movies:
1966 (International)

Shorts:
Your Career: Your Decision? (1976) Educational

Run, Light Buck, Run (1966)

Walt Disney's Wonderful World of Color

Source:
Run, Light Buck, Run! (1962) B.F. Beebe

Writers:
Jack Couffer

Director:
Jack Couffer

Stars:
Al Niemela

Broadcast:
Mar 13, 1966, NBC

Length:
50 min

Concho, the Coyote Who Wasn't (1966)

Walt Disney's Wonderful World of Color

Writers:
Inez Cocke, Jack Couffer

Director:
Jack Couffer

Broadcast:
Apr 10, 1966, NBC

Length:
50 min

The Legend of El Blanco (1966)

Walt Disney's Wonderful World of Color

Source:
El Blanco: The Legend of the White Stallion (1961) Rutherford Montgomery

Writers:
Homer McCoy, Jack Speirs

Director:
Arthur J. Vitarelli

Stars:
Alfonso Romero, Jose F. Perez

Broadcast:
Sep 25, 1966, NBC

Length:
50 min

The 101 Problems of Hercules (1966)

Walt Disney's Wonderful World of Color

Writers:
Rod Peterson (screenplay), Tom McGowan (story)

Director:
Tom Boutross

Broadcast:
Oct 16, 1966, NBC

Length:
50 min

Video:
1994 *The Wonderful World of Disney: Run, Appaloosa, Run*

Gallegher Goes West (1966-1967)

Walt Disney's Wonderful World of Color

Source:
Follows *The Further Adventures of Gallegher* (1965)

Episodes:
Showdown with the Sundown Kid (Part 1), *Crusading Reporter* (Part 2), *Tragedy on the Trail* (Part 3), *Trial by Terror* (Part 4)

Writers:
Maurice Tombragel

Directors:
Joseph Sargent (Parts 1 & 2), James Sheldon (Parts 3 & 4)

Stars:
Dennis Weaver, John McIntire, Roger Mobley, Ray Teal

Broadcast:
Oct 23, 1966 (Part 1), Oct 30, 1966 (Part 2), Jan 29, 1967 (Part 3), Feb 5, 1967 (Part 4), NBC

Length:
4 x 50 min

A Ranger's Guide to Nature (1966)

Walt Disney's Wonderful World of Color

Writers:
Ted Berman

Director:
Hamilton S. Luske

Broadcast:
Nov 13, 1966, NBC

Length:
50 min

Video:
1990s *The Plausible Impossible*

Soundtrack:
1966 *A Nature Guide about Birds, Bees, Beavers, and Bears* (LP)

Joker, the Amiable Ocelot (1966)

Walt Disney's Wonderful World of Color

Writers:
Rod Peterson (screenplay), Robert Becker (story)

Stars:
Robert Becker, Jan McNabb

Broadcast:
Dec 11, 1966, NBC

Length:
50 min

Video:
1990s *Wonderful World of Disney: Nature's Better Built Homes*

Disneyland Around the Seasons (1966)

Walt Disney's Wonderful World of Color

Writers:
Larry Clemmons

Director:
Hamilton S. Luske

Broadcast:
Dec 18, 1966, NBC

Length:
51 min

Shorts:
1967 (International)

DVD:
2007 *WD Treasures: Disneyland: Secrets, Stories & Magic*

Digital:
Amazon

Willie and the Yank (1967)

Walt Disney's Wonderful World of Color

AKA:
Mosby's Marauders (International)

Episodes:
The Deserter (Part 1), *Mosby Raiders* (Part 2), *The Matchmaker* (Part 3)

Writers:
Harold Swanton

Director:
Michael O'Herlihy

Stars:
James MacArthur, Nick Adams, Kurt Russell, Jack Ging

Broadcast:
Jan 8, 1967 (Part 1), Jan 15, 1967 (Part 2), Jan 22, 1967 (Part 3), NBC
Length:
79 min (feature), 3 x 50 min (episodes)
Movies:
1967 (International)
Video:
1987 *Mosby's Marauders*

The Boy Who Flew with Condors (1967)
Walt Disney's Wonderful World of Color
Source:
The Sail Plane Story (?) Ken Nelson
Writers:
Homer McCoy
Director:
James Algar
Stars:
Christopher Jury, Margaret Birsner, Fred W. Harris
Broadcast:
Feb 19, 1967, NBC
Length:
49 min
DVD:
2008 Disney Movie Club Exclusive

Atta Girl, Kelly! (1967)
Walt Disney's Wonderful World of Color
Episodes:
K for Kelly (Part 1), *Dog of Destiny* (Part 2), *The Seeing Eye* (Part 3)
Writers:
Albert Aley
Director:
James Sheldon
Stars:
Billy Corcoran, Beau Bridges, Arthur Hill, J.D. Cannon
Broadcast:
Mar 5, 1967 (Part 1), Mar 12, 1967 (Part 2), Mar 19, 1967 (Part 3), NBC

Length:
139 min
DVD:
2009 Disney Movie Club Exclusive

Man on Wheels (1967)
Walt Disney's Wonderful World of Color
Includes:
Donald and the Wheel (1961), *Freewayphobia #1* (1965)
Writers:
Bill Berg, William R. Bosché
Director:
Hamilton S. Luske
Broadcast:
Mar 26, 1967, NBC
Length:
50 min
Video:
1990s *The Wonderful World of Disney: Pacifically Peeking with Moby Duck*

A Salute to Alaska (1967)
Walt Disney's Wonderful World of Color
Writers:
Bill Berg, Norman Wright
Directors:
Hamilton S. Luske, Ward Kimball
Broadcast:
Apr 2, 1967, NBC
Length:
50 min

The Not So Lonely Lighthouse Keeper (1967)
Walt Disney's Wonderful World of Color
Writers:
Jack Couffer
Director:
Jack Couffer
Stars:
Clarence Hastings, Ingrid Niemela

Broadcast:
Sep 17, 1967, NBC
Length:
50 min

How the West Was Lost (1967)
Walt Disney's Wonderful World of Color
Includes:
El Gaucho Goofy (1943), *Pecos Bill* (1948), *Two Gun Goofy* (1952)
Writers:
Ted Berman, Otto Englander
Director:
Hamilton S. Luske
Broadcast:
Sep 24, 1967, NBC
Length:
50 min

One Day on Beetle Rock (1967)
Walt Disney's Wonderful World of Color
Source:
One Day on Beetle Rock (1944) Sally Carrighar
Director:
James Algar
Broadcast:
Nov 19, 1967
Length:
50 min
Shorts:
A Day in Nature's Community (1975) Educational, edited from episode

A Boy Called Nuthin' (1967)
Walt Disney's Wonderful World of Color
Source:
Nuthin' (1952) Harry E. Webb
Writers:
Lowell S. Hawley, James Leighton
Director:
Norman Tokar

Stars:
Forrest Tucker, Ronny Howard, John Carroll, Mary La Roche

Broadcast:
Dec 10, 1967 (Part 1), Dec 17, 1967 (Part 2), NBC

Length:
2 x 50 min

Way Down Cellar (1968)

Walt Disney's Wonderful World of Color

Source:
Way Down Cellar (1942) Phil Strong

Director:
Robert Totten

Stars:
Butch Patrick, Sheldon Collins, Lundy Davis, Frank McHugh

Broadcast:
Jan 7, 1968 (Part 1), Jan 14, 1968 (Part 2), NBC

Length:
2 x 50 min

From the Pirates of the Caribbean to the World of Tomorrow (1968)

Walt Disney's Wonderful World of Color

AKA:
Disneyland: From the Pirates of the Caribbean to the World of Tomorrow

Source:
Behind the scenes at Disneyland

Writers:
Marty Sklar

Director:
Hamilton S. Luske

Broadcast:
Jan 21, 1968, NBC

Length:
50 min

DVD/Blu-ray:
2003/2004 *Pirates of the Caribbean: The Curse of the Black Pearl* (18 min excerpt)

Pablo and the Dancing Chihuahua (1968)

Walt Disney's Wonderful World of Color

Writers:
Paul Lucey, Jack Speirs (screenplay), Homer Brightman (story)
Director:
Walter Perkins
Stars:
Armando Islas, Francesca Jarvis, Walker Tilley, Manuel Rivera
Broadcast:
Jan 28, 1968 (Part 1), Feb 4, 1968 (Part 2), NBC
Length:
2 x 50 min
Movies:
1969 (International)

My Family is a Menagerie (1968)

Walt Disney's Wonderful World of Color

Stars:
Ann Harrell, Jack Garrity, Kathy Thorn
Broadcast:
Feb 11, 1968, NBC
Length:
50 min

The Young Loner (1968)

Walt Disney's Wonderful World of Color

Source:
The Loner (1963) Ester Wier
Writers:
Lowell S. Hawley
Director:
Michael O'Herlihy
Stars:
Kim Hunter, Frank Silvera, Butch Patrick, Edward Andrews
Broadcast:
Feb 25, 1968 (Part 1), Mar 3, 1968 (Part 2), NBC
Length:
2 x 50 min

Wild Heart (1968)

Walt Disney's Wonderful World of Color

Writers:
Jack Couffer

Director:
Jack Couffer

Stars:
Andrew Penn, Kitty Porteous, Stanley Bowles

Broadcast:
Mar 10, 1968, NBC

Length:
50 min

Shorts:
Nature's Wild Heart (1973) Educational

The Ranger of Brownstone (1968)

Walt Disney's Wonderful World of Color

Includes:
Rugged Bear (1953), *Grin and Bear It* (1954), *Bearly Asleep* (1955), *Beezy Bear* (1955), *Hooked Bear* (1956), *In the Bag* (1956)

Writers:
Ted Berman, Al Bertino, David Detiege

Director:
Hamilton S. Luske

Broadcast:
Mar 17, 1968, NBC

Length:
50 min

Video:
1990s *The Wonderful World of Disney: The Ranger of Brownstone*

The Mystery of Edward Sims (1968)

Walt Disney's Wonderful World of Color

Source:
Follows *Gallegher Goes West* (1966-1967)

Writers:
Hermon Groves

Director:
Seymour Robbie

Stars:
Roger Mobley, John McIntire, John Dehner, Warren Oates
Broadcast:
Mar 31, 1968 (Part 1), Apr 7, 1968 (Part 2), NBC
Length:
50 min (episode)

Nature's Charter Tours (1968)
Walt Disney's Wonderful World of Color
Writers:
Ted Berman (story), Mel Leven (narration)
Director:
Hamilton S. Luske
Broadcast:
Apr 28, 1968, NBC
Length:
2 x 50 mins

Boomerang, Dog of Many Talents (1968)
Walt Disney's Wonderful World of Color
Director:
John Newland
Stars:
Darren McGavin, Patricia Crowley, Darby Hinton, Lori Farrow
Broadcast:
Sep 22, 1968 (Part 1), Sep 29, 1968 (Part 2), NBC
Length:
2 x 50 min

Pacifically Peeking (1968)
Walt Disney's Wonderful World of Color
Writers:
Bill Berg (story), Mel Leven (narration)
Director:
Ward Kimball
Broadcast:
Oct 6, 1968, NBC
Length:
50 min

Comic Books:
Moby Duck on "Jinx Island" (Walt Disney Showcase #2, Jan 1971)
Video:
1990s The Wonderful World of Disney Pacifically Peeking with Moby Duck

Brimstone, the Amish Horse (1968)

Walt Disney's Wonderful World of Color

Writers:
William J. Bryan
Director:
Larry Lansburgh
Stars:
Pamela Toll, Wallace Rooney, Phil Clark, Robert Allen
Broadcast:
Oct 27, 1968, NBC
Length:
50 min

The Treasure of San Bosco Reef (1968)

Walt Disney's Wonderful World of Color

Writers:
Maurice Tombragel
Director:
Robert L. Friend
Stars:
Roger Mobley, James Daly, Nehemiah Persoff, John van Dreelen, Antony Alda
Broadcast:
Nov 24, 1968 (Part 1), Dec 1, 1968 (Part 2), NBC
Length:
2 x 50 min

The Owl That Didn't Give a Hoot (1968)

Walt Disney's Wonderful World of Color

Director:
Frank Zuniga
Stars:
David Potter, Marian Fletcher, John Fetzer, Hyde Clayton

Broadcast:
Dec 15, 1968, NBC

Length:
50 min

The Mickey Mouse Anniversary Show (1968)

Walt Disney's Wonderful World of Color

Source:
Various Mickey Mouse shorts

Writers:
Ward Kimball

Director:
Robert Stevenson

Broadcast:
Dec 22, 1968, NBC

Length:
50 min (Original), 84 min (Theatrical)

Movies:
1970 (Europe)

Laserdisc:
1987 (Japan)

Solomon, the Sea Turtle (1969)

Walt Disney's Wonderful World of Color

Source:
The Windward Road (1956) Archie Carr

Stars:
Dr. Archie Carr, Henry Del Giudice, Steve Weinstock, Arthur Holgate

Broadcast:
Jan 5, 1969, NBC

Length:
50 min

Pancho, the Fastest Paw in the West (1969)

Walt Disney's Wonderful World of Color

Source:
Pancho, a Dog of the Plains (1958) Bruce Grant

Stars:
Armando Islas, Frank Keith, Albert Hachmeister

Broadcast:
Feb 2, 1969, NBC

Length:
50 min

The Secret of Boyne Castle (1969)

Walt Disney's Wonderful World of Color

AKA:
Guns in the Heather (Theatrical), *Spy-Busters* (rerun)

Source:
Guns in the Heather (1963) Lockhart Amerman

Writers:
Herman Groves

Director:
Robert Butler

Stars:
Glenn Corbert, Kurt Russell, Alfred Burke, Patrick Dawson

Broadcast:
Feb 9, 1969 (Part 1), Feb 16, 1969 (Part 2), Feb 23, 1969 (Part 3), NBC

Length:
3 x 50 min (episodes), 89 min (feature)

Movies:
1969 *Guns in the Heather (Europe)*

Nature's Better Built Homes (1969)

Walt Disney's Wonderful World of Color

Writers:
Ted Berman (story), Mel Leven (narration)

Directors:
Ward Kimball, Hamilton S. Luske

Broadcast:
Mar 2, 1969, NBC

Length:
50 min

Video:
1990s *The Wonderful World of Disney: Nature's Better Built Homes*

Ride a Northbound Horse (1969)

Walt Disney's Wonderful World of Color

Source:
Ride a Northbound Horse (1964) Richard Edward Wormser

Writers:
Herman Groves

Director:
Robert Totten

Stars:
Carroll O'Connor, Michael Shea, Ben Johnson, Dub Taylor

Broadcast:
Mar 16, 1969 (Part 1), Mar 23, 1969 (Part 2), NBC

Length:
2 x 50 min

Movies:
1969 (Europe)

Wild Geese Calling (1969)

The Wonderful World of Disney

Source:
Wild Geese Calling (1966) Robert Murphy

Director:
James Algar

Stars:
Carl Draper, Persis Overton

Broadcast:
Sep 14, 1969, NBC

Length:
50 min

Shorts:
1971 (International)

My Dog, the Thief (1969)

The Wonderful World of Disney

Writers:
Gordon Buford (story), William Raynor, Myles Wilder (screenplay)

Director:
Robert Stevenson

Stars:
Dwayne Hickman, Mary Ann Mobley, Elsa Lanchester, Joe Flynn

Broadcast:
Sep 21, 1969 (Part 1), Sep 28, 1969 (Part 2), NBC

Length:
2 x 50 min (episodes), 88 min (feature)

Comic Strips:
My Dog, the Thief (TCT, Sep 7—Nov 30, 1969)

DVD:
2006

The Feather Farm (1969)

The Wonderful World of Disney

Stars:
Nick Nolte, Mel Weiser, Christine Coates, Shirley Fabricant

Broadcast:
Oct 26, 1969, NBC

Length:
50 min

Varda, the Peregrine Falcon (1969)

The Wonderful World of Disney

Director:
Frank Zuniga

Stars:
Peter de Manio, Noreen Klincko, Denise Grisco

Broadcast:
Nov 16, 1969, NBC

Length:
50 min

Secrets of the Pirates' Inn (1969)

The Wonderful World of Disney

Source:
The Secrets of the Pirate Inn (1968) Wylly Folk St. John

Writers:
Herman Groves

Director:
Gary Nelson

Stars:
Ed Begley, Jimmy Bracken, Annie McEveety, Patrick Creamer
Broadcast:
Nov 23, 1969 (Part 1), Nov 30, 1969 (Part 2), NBC
Length:
2 x 50 min

Inky the Crow (1969)

The Wonderful World of Disney

Stars:
Deborah Bainbridge, Margo Lungreen, Willard Granger, Rowan Pease
Broadcast:
Dec 7, 1969, NBC
Length:
50 min

PART FOUR

1970–1974

Smoke (1970)

The Wonderful World of Disney

Source:
Smoke (1967) William Corbin

Writers:
John Furia, Jr.

Director:
Vincent McEveety

Stars:
Earl Holliman, Ronny Howard, Jacqueline Scott, Shug Fisher

Broadcast:
Feb 1, 1970 (Part 1), Feb 8, 1970 (Part 2), NBC

Length:
2 x 50 min (episodes), 90 min (feature)

Movies:
1970 (UK)

Shorts:
Stepparents: Where Is the Love? (1975) Educational

Video:
1986, 1997

Menace on the Mountain (1970)

The Wonderful World of Disney

Source:
Menace on the Mountain (1968) Mary A. Hancock

Writers:
Robert Heverly

Director:
Vincent McEveety

Stars:
Mitch Vogel, Charles Aidman, Patricia Crowley, Albery Salmi

Broadcast:
Mar 1, 1970 (Part 1), Mar 8, 1970 (Part 2), NBC

Length:
2 x 50 min (episodes), 81 min (feature)

Movies:
1972 (UK)

Video:
1986

DVD:
2011 Disney Movie Club Exclusive

Disneyland Showtime (1970)

The Wonderful World of Disney

Source:
Behind the scenes of Disneyland and The Haunted Mansion

Writers:
John Bradford, Jim De Foe, Ed Haas, Bill Richmond

Director:
Gordon Wiles

Broadcast:
Mar 22, 1970, NBC

Length:
50 min

Nature's Strangest Oddballs (1970)

The Wonderful World of Disney

Source:
The Cold-Blooded Penguin (1945), *Goliath II* (1960), *Nature's Strangest Creatures* (1959)

Writers:
Ted Berman, Otto Englander, Bill Peet

Directors:
Les Clark, Hamilton S. Luske

Broadcast:
Mar 29, 1970, NBC

Length:
50 min

Cristobalito, the Calypso Colt (1970)

The Wonderful World of Disney

Writers:
Norman Wright

Director:
Norman Wright

Stars:
Roberto Vigoreaux, Walter Buso

Broadcast:
Sep 13, 1970, NBC

Length:
47 min

DVD:
2012 Generations Collection

The Boy Who Stole the Elephant (1970)

The Wonderful World of Disney

Source:
The Boy Who Stole the Elephant (1952) Julilly H. Kohler

Writers:
William Robert Yates, John McGreevey

Director:
Michael Caffey

Stars:
Mark Lester, David Wayne, June Havoc, Dabbs Greer

Broadcast:
Sep 20, 1970 (Part 1), Sep 27, 1970 (Part 2), NBC

Length:
95 min (feature), 2 x 50 min (episodes)

DVD:
2012 Generations Collection

The Wacky Zoo of Morgan City (1970)

The Wonderful World of Disney

Source:
I'll Trade You an Elk (1967) Charles A. Goodrum

Writers:
Joseph L. McEveety

Director:
Marvin J. Chomsky

Stars:
Hal Holbrook, Joe Flynn, Cecil Kellaway, Wally Cox

Broadcast:
Oct 18, 1970 (Part 1), Oct 25, 1970 (Part 2), NBC

Length:
2 x 50 min

Snow Bear (1970)

The Wonderful World of Disney

Director:
Gunther von Fritsch

Stars:
Steve Kalcak, Rossman Peetook, Laura Itta, Dan Truesdell

Broadcast:
Nov 1, 1970 (Part 1), Nov 8, 1970 (Part 2), NBC

Length:
2 x 50 min

Shorts:
1972 *Track of the Giant Snow Bear* (16mm)

Three Without Fear (1971)

The Wonderful World of Disney

Episodes:
Lost on the Baja Peninsula (Part 1), *In the Land of the Desert Whales* (Part 2)

Source:
Three Without Fear (1969) Robert C. Du Soe

Director:
Frank Zuniga

Stars:
Bart Orlando, Pablo Lopez, Marion Valjalo, Claude Earls

Broadcast:
Jan 3, 1971 (Part 1), Jan 10, 1971 (Part 2), NBC

Length:
2 x 50 min

Bayou Boy (1971)

The Wonderful World of Disney

AKA:
The Boy From Deadman's Bayou

Writers:
Louis Pelletier

Director:
Gary Nelson

Stars:
John McIntire, Mitch Vogel, Mike Lookinland, Jeanette Nolan

Broadcast:
Feb 7, 1971 (Part 1), Feb 14, 1971 (Part 2), NBC

Length:
2 x 50 min

Hamad and the Pirates (1971)

The Wonderful World of Disney

Episodes:
The Phantom Dhow (Part 1), *The Island of the Three Palms* (Part 2)

Writers:
Gerald Pearce (screenplay), Richard H. Lyford (story)

Director:
Richard H. Lyford

Stars:
Khalik Marshad, Abdullah Masoud, Kalifah Shaheen, Mubarak Buzaid

Broadcast:
Mar 7, 1971 (Part 1), Mar 14, 1971 (Part 2), NBC

Length:
2 x 50 min

Charlie Crowfoot and the Coati Mundi (1971)

The Wonderful World of Disney

Stars:
Edward Colunga, Robert Keyworth

Broadcast:
Sep 19, 1971, NBC

Length:
50 min

Hacksaw (1971)

The Wonderful World of Disney

Writers:
Dick Spencer III (screenplay), Larry Lansburgh (story)

Director:
Larry Lansburgh

Stars:
Tab Hunter, Susan Bracken, Victor Millan, Ray Teal

Broadcast:
Sep 26, 1971 (Part 1), Oct 3, 1971 (Part 2)

Length:
89 min (feature), 2 x 50 min (episodes)

Digital:
Amazon, iTunes, Vudu

The Strange Monster of Strawberry Cove (1971)

The Wonderful World of Disney

Source:
The Strange Sea Monster of Strawberry Lake (1960) Bertrand R. Brinley

Writers:
Herman Groves

Director:
Jack Shea

Stars:
Burgess Meredith, Agnes Moorehead, Annie McEveety, Jimmy Bracken

Broadcast:
Oct 31, 1971 (Part 1), Nov 7, 1971 (Part 2), NBC

Length:
2 x 50 min

Lefty, the Dingaling Lynx (1971)

The Wonderful World of Disney

Writers:
Jack Speirs

Director:
Winston Hibler

Stars:
Ron Brown, Harrison Tout, Brooks Woolley, Elaine Ayres
Broadcast:
Nov 28, 1971 (Part 1), Dec 5, 1971 (Part 2), NBC
Length:
2 x 50 min

Disney on Parade (1971)

The Wonderful World of Disney

Source:
Disney on Parade (1969-1974) arena show
Director:
Stan Harris
Broadcast:
Dec 19, 1971, NBC
Length:
50 min

Mountain Born (1972)

The Wonderful World of Disney

Source:
Mountain Born (1943) Elizabeth Yates
Director:
James Algar
Stars:
Sam Austin, Walter Stroud, Jolene Terry
Broadcast:
Jan 9, 1972, NBC
Length:
50 min

Justin Morgan Had a Horse (1972)

The Wonderful World of Disney

Source:
Justin Morgan Had a Horse (1945) Marguerite Henry
Writers:
Calvin Clements Jr., Rod Peterson
Director:
Hollingsworth Morse

Stars:
Don Murray, Lana Wood, Gary Crosby, R.G. Armstrong

Broadcast:
Feb 6, 1972 (Part 1), Feb 13, 1972 (Part 2), NBC

Length:
91 min (feature), 2 x 50 min (episodes)

Video:
1982

DVD:
2012 Generations Collection

Digital:
Amazon, iTunes, Vudu

The City Fox (1972)
The Wonderful World of Disney

Director:
James Algar

Stars:
Tom Chan, Jerry Jerish

Broadcast:
Feb 20, 1972, NBC

Length:
50 min

Chango, Guardian of the Mayan Treasure (1972)
The Wonderful World of Disney

Source:
Yucatan Monkey (1967) B.F. Beebe

Stars:
Alonzo Fuentes, Juan Maldonado, Alex Tinne

Broadcast:
Mar 19, 1972, NBC

Length:
50 min

Michael O'Hara the Fourth (1972)

The Wonderful World of Disney

Episodes:
To Trap a Thief (Part 1), *The Deceptive Detective* (Part 2)

Director:
Robert Totten

Stars:
Jo Ann Harris, Dan Dailey, Michael McGreevey, Nehemiah Persoff

Broadcast:
Mar 26, 1972 (Part 1), Apr 2, 1972 (Part 2)

Length:
2 x 50 min

The Nashville Coyote (1972)

The Wonderful World of Disney

Director:
Winston Hibler

Stars:
Walter Forbes, William Garton, Eugene Scott, Michael Edwards

Broadcast:
Oct 1, 1972, NBC

Length:
50 min

Soundtrack:
1973 *Walt Disney Production's Nashville Coyote* (LP)

The High Flying Spy (1972)

The Wonderful World of Disney

Director:
Vincent McEveety

Stars:
Stuart Whitman, Vincent Van Patten, Darren McGavin, Andrew Prine

Broadcast:
Oct 22, 1972 (Part 1), Oct 29, 1972 (Part 2), Nov 5, 1972 (Part 3), NBC

Length:
3 x 50 min

Nosey, the Sweetest Skunk in the World (1972)

The Wonderful World of Disney

Stars:
Jane Biddle, James Chandler, Walter Carlson, Lois Binford

Broadcast:
Nov 19, 1972, NBC

Length:
50 min

Chandar, the Black Leopard of Ceylon (1972)

The Wonderful World of Disney

Writers:
William Robert Yates

Director:
Winston Hibler

Stars:
Frederick Steyne, Esram Jayasinghe, Joe Abeywickrama

Broadcast:
Nov 26, 1972 (Part 1), Dec 3, 1972 (Part 2), NBC

Length:
2 x 50 min

Salty, the Hijacked Harbor Seal (1972)

The Wonderful World of Disney

Director:
Harry Tytle

Stars:
John Waugh, Doug Grey, Lance Rasmussen, Bud Sheble

Broadcast:
Dec 17, 1972, NBC

Length:
50 min

The Mystery in Dracula's Castle (1973)

The Wonderful World of Disney

Writers:
Sue Milburn

Director:
Robert Totten

Stars:
Clu Gulager, Mariette Hartley, Johnny Whitaker, Scott Kolden
Broadcast:
Jan 7, 1973 (Part 1), Jan 14, 1973 (Part 2), NBC
Length:
2 x 50 min

50 Happy Years (1973)
The Wonderful World of Disney
AKA:
Fifty Happy Years
Broadcast:
Jan 21, 1973, NBC
Length:
50 min
Soundtrack:
1973 *50 Happy Years of Disney Favorites* (LP)

Chester, Yesterday's Horse (1973)
The Wonderful World of Disney
Director:
Larry Lansburgh
Stars:
Bill Williams, Barbara Hale, Russ McGubbin, Jerry Gatlin
Broadcast:
Mar 4, 1973, NBC
Length:
50 min

The Little Shepherd Dog of Catalina (1973)
The Wonderful World of Disney
Director:
Harry Tytle
Stars:
Clint Rowe, William Maxwell, Joe Dawkins, Robert O'Guin
Broadcast:
Mar 11, 1973, NBC
Length:
50 min

The Boy and the Bronc Buster (1973)

The Wonderful World of Disney

Director:
Bernard McEveety

Stars:
Earl Holliman, Strother Martin, Vincent Van Patten, Jacqueline Scott

Broadcast:
Mar 18, 1973 (Part 1), Mar 25, 1973 (Part 2), NBC

Length:
2 x 50 min

Call It Courage (1973)

The Wonderful World of Disney

Source:
Call It Courage (1940) Armstrong Sperry

Writers:
Ben Masselink

Director:
Roy Edward Disney

Stars:
Evan Temarii

Broadcast:
Apr 1, 1973, NBC

Length:
48 min

DVD:
2011 Disney Movie Club Exclusive

Fire on Kelly Mountain (1973)

The Wonderful World of Disney

Source:
The Mallory Burn (1971) 'Pete Pomeroy' (Arthur J. Roth)

Writers:
Calvin Clements Jr.

Director:
William Beaudine Jr.

Stars:
Andrew Duggan, Larry Wilcox, Anne Lockhart, Noam Pitlik

Broadcast:
Sep 30, 1973, NBC
Length:
50 min
Video:
1988 *The Wonderful World of Disney: Fire on Kelly Mountain*

Mustang! (1973)
The Wonderful World of Disney
Writer:
Calvin Clements
Director:
Roy Edward Disney (Part 1), Frank Zuniga (Part 2)
Stars:
Charles Baca, Flavio Martinez, Ignacio Ramirez, Alfonso Cantu
Broadcast:
Oct 7, 1973 (Part 1), Oct 21, 1973 (Part 2), NBC
Length:
2 x 50 min

The Proud Bird from Shanghai (1973)
The Wonderful World of Disney
Source:
Based on a true story
Writers:
Joe Ansen
Director:
Harry Tytle
Broadcast:
Dec 16, 1973, NBC
Length:
50 min

The Whiz Kid and the Mystery at Riverton (1974)
The Wonderful World of Disney
Source:
Alvin Fernald, Mayor for a Day (1970) Clifford B. Hicks

Writers:
Herman Groves

Director:
Tom Leetch

Stars:
Edward Andrews, John Fiedler, Eric Shea, Clay O'Brien

Broadcast:
Jan 6, 1974 (Part 1), Jan 13, 1974 (Part 2), NBC

Length:
2 x 50 min

TV Anthology:
The Whiz Kid and the Carnival Caper (1976) Sequel

Hog Wild (1974)

The Wonderful World of Disney

Source:
Hog Wild! (1961) Julia Brown Ridle

Writers:
Gabe Essoe

Director:
Jerome Courtland

Stars:
John Ericson, Diana Muldaur, Clay O'Brien, Nicholas Beauvy

Broadcast:
Jan 20, 1974 (Part 1), Jan 27, 1974 (Part 2), NBC

Length:
2 x 50 min

Carlo, the Sierra Coyote (1974)

The Wonderful World of Disney

Writers:
Homer McCoy

Director:
James Algar

Stars:
Jana Milo, Steven S. Stewart, Hal Bokar, Dale Alexander

Broadcast:
Feb 3, 1974, NBC

Length:
50 min

Ringo, the Refugee Raccoon (1974)

The Wonderful World of Disney

Writers:
Barry Clark

Director:
Roy Edward Disney

Stars:
William Hochstrasser

Broadcast:
Mar 3, 1974, NBC

Length:
50 min

Diamonds on Wheels (1974)

The Wonderful World of Disney

Source:
Nightmare Rally (1965) Pierre Castex

Writers:
William R. Yates

Director:
Jerome Courtland

Stars:
Patrick Allen, Peter Firth, George Sewell, Spencer Banks

Broadcast:
Mar 10, 1974 (Part 1), Mar 17, 1974 (Part 2), Mar 24, 1974 (Part 3), NBC

Length:
3 x 50 min (episodes), 84 min (feature)

Movies:
1973 (UK)

Video:
1987

Shokee, the Everglades Panther (1974)

The Wonderful World of Disney

Director:
Roy Edward Disney

Stars:
Curtis Osceola

Broadcast:
Seo 29, 1974, NBC

Length:
50 min

Return of the Big Cat (1974)

The Wonderful World of Disney

Source:
The Year of the Big Cat (1970) Lew Dietz

Writers:
Herman Groves

Director:
Tom Leetch

Stars:
Christian Juttner, Jeremy Slate, Patricia Crowley, David Wayne

Broadcast:
Oct 6, 1974 (Part 1), Oct 13, 1974 (Part 2), NBC

Length:
2 x 50 min

Movies:
1975 (International)

Two Against the Arctic (1974)

The Wonderful World of Disney

Director:
Robert Clouse

Stars:
Susie Silook, Marty Smith, Rossman Peetook

Broadcast:
Oct 20, 1974 (Part 1), Oct 27, 1974 (Part 2), NBC

Length:
2 x 50 min

Adventure in Satan's Canyon (1974)

The Wonderful World of Disney

Writers:
Shane Tatum, James Douglass West

Director:
William Beaudine Jr.

Stars:
Richard Jaeckel, David Alan Bailey, Larry Pennell

Broadcast:
Nov 3, 1974, NBC

Length:
50 min

Video:
1988 *The Wonderful World of Disney: Fire on Kelly Mountain*

Runaway on the Rogue River (1974)

The Wonderful World of Disney

Writers:
Larry Lansburgh Jr., Brian Lansburgh (screenplay), Larry Lansburgh (story)

Director:
Larry Lansburgh

Stars:
Slim Pickens, Willie Aames, Denis Arndt

Broadcast:
Dec 1, 1974, NBC

Length:
50 min

Video:
1986 *The Wonderful World of Disney: The Bluegrass Specials*

PART FIVE

1975–1979

The Sky's the Limit (1975)

The Wonderful World of Disney

Writers:
Harry Spalding (screenplay), Larry Lenville (story)
Director:
Tom Leetch
Stars:
Pat O'Brien, Lloyd Nolan, Ike Eisenmann, Jeanette Nolan
Broadcast:
Jan 19, 1975 (Part 1), Jan 26, 1975 (Part 2), NBC
Length:
2 x 50 min

The Footloose Goose (1975)

The Wonderful World of Disney

Director:
James Algar
Stars:
Brett Hadley, Paul Preston, Judy Bement
Broadcast:
Mar 9, 1975, NBC
Length:
50 min

Deacon, the High Noon Dog (1975)

The Wonderful World of Disney

Writers:
Norman Wright

Director:
Norman Wright

Stars:
Frank Keith, Paul Szemenyei, C. Gordon Smith

Broadcast:
Mar 16, 1975, NBC

Length:
50 min

Welcome to the "World" (1975)

The Wonderful World of Disney

Source:
Opening of Space Mountain at Walt Disney World

Writers:
Sheldon Keller

Director:
Marty Pasetta

Broadcast:
Mar 23, 1975, NBC

Length:
50 min

The Boy Who Talked to Badgers (1975)

The Wonderful World of Disney

Source:
Based on a true story

Director:
Gary Nelson

Stars:
Christian Juttner, Carl Betz, Salome Jens, Denver Pyle

Broadcast:
Sep 14, 1975 (Part 1), Sep 21, 1975 (Part 2), NBC

Length:
2 x 50 min

The Outlaw Cats of Colossal Cave (1975)

The Wonderful World of Disney

Director:
Hank Schloss

Stars:
Gilbert de la Peña, José Maierhauser

Broadcast:
Sep 28, 1975, NBC

Length:
50 min

The Secret of the Pond (1975)

The Wonderful World of Disney

Director:
Robert Day

Stars:
Anthony Zerbe, Ike Eisenmann, Eric Shea, John McLiam

Broadcast:
Oct 5, 1975 (Part 1), Oct 12, (Part 2), NBC

Length:
2 x 50 min

Seems There Was This Moose (1975)

The Wonderful World of Disney

Director:
Roy Edward Disney

Stars:
Bob Cox, Ron Brown

Broadcast:
Oct 19, 1975, NBC

Length:
50 min

Twister, Bull from the Sky (1976)

The Wonderful World of Disney

Director:
Larry Lansburgh

Stars:
Larry Wilcox, Willie Aames, Keith Andes, Denis Arndt

Broadcast:
Jan 4, 1976, NBC

Length:
50 min

The Whiz Kid and the Carnival Caper (1976)

The Wonderful World of Disney

Source:
Sequel to *The Whiz Kid and the Mystery at Riverton* (1974)

Writers:
Tom Leetch, Jan Williams (story), Herman Groves (story/screenplay)

Director:
Tom Leetch

Stars:
Jack Kruschen, John Colicos, Jaclyn Smith, Eric Shea

Broadcast:
Jan 11, 1976 (Part 1), Jan 18, 1976 (Part 2), NBC

Length:
2 x 50 min

The Survival of Sam the Pelican (1976)

The Wonderful World of Disney

Writers:
Ben Masselink, Norman Wright

Director:
Roy Edward Disney

Stars:
Kim Friese, Scott Lee, Bill DeHollander

Broadcast:
Feb 29, 1976, NBC

Length:
50 min

The Flight of the Grey Wolf (1976)

The Wonderful World of Disney

Source:
Flight of the White Wolf (1970) Mel Ellis

Writers:
Calvin Clements, Jr.

Director:
Frank Zuniga

Stars:
Jeff East, Bill Williams, Barbara Hale, William Bryant

Broadcast:
Mar 14, 1976 (Part 1), Mar 21, 1976 (Part 2), NBC
Length:
2 x 50 min (episodes), 82 min (feature)
Video:
1997
DVD:
2011 Disney Movie Club Exclusive

Superstar Goofy (1976)

The Wonderful World of Disney
Source:
Various Goofy shorts (1939-1961)
Broadcast:
Jul 25, 1976, NBC
Length:
74 min
Movie:
1972 (Europe)

The Secret of Old Glory Mine (1976)

The Wonderful World of Disney
Director:
Fred R. Krug
Stars:
Rowan Pease, Barry Dowell
Broadcast:
Oct 31, 1976, NBC
Length:
50 min

Disney's Greatest Dog Stars (1976)

The Wonderful World of Disney
Source:
Behind the scenes of *The Shaggy D.A.* (1976)
Broadcast:
Nov 28, 1976, NBC
Length:
50 min

Laserdisc:
Japan

The Golden Dog (1977)

The Wonderful World of Disney

Writers:
William Canning, Norman Wright

Directors:
William Stierwalt, Fred R. Krug

Stars:
Paul Brinegar, Alan Napier

Broadcast:
Jan 2, 1977, NBC

Length:
50 min

Kit Carson and the Mountain Men (1977)

The Wonderful World of Disney

Source:
Life of Kit Carson (1809-1868)

Director:
Vincent McEveety

Stars:
Christopher Connelly, Robert Reed, Ike Eisenmann, Gary Lockwood

Broadcast:
Jan 9, 1977 (Part 1), Jan 16, 1977 (Part 2)

Length:
2 x 50 min

Barry of the Great St. Bernard (1977)

The Wonderful World of Disney

Source:
Novel by Adolf Fux

Writers:
Sheldon Stark, Ann Udell (screenplay), Tom Seller (adaptation), Joe Ansen (narration)

Director:
Frank Zuniga

Stars:
Jean Claude Dauphin, Pierre Tabard, Maurice Teynac, Pascale Christophe

Broadcast:
Jan 30, 1977 (Part 1), Feb 6, 1977 (Part 2)

Length:
2 x 50 min (episodes), 91 min (feature)

DVD:
2012 Generations Collection

The Mystery of Rustler's Cave (1977)
The New Mickey Mouse Club

Director:
Tom Leetch

Stars:
Kim Richards, Robbie Rist, Christian Juttner, Bobby Rolofson

Broadcast:
Feb 1—Mar 1, 1977

Length:
Unknown (Serial)

Go West, Young Dog (1977)
The Wonderful World of Disney

Director:
William Stierwalt

Stars:
Frank Keith, Charles Granata, Dennis Dillon, Donald Harris

Broadcast:
Feb 20, 1977, NBC

Length:
50 min

The Ghost of Cypress Swamp (1977)
The Wonderful World of Disney

Source:
Weakfoot: The Ghost of Cramer's Island (1975) Linda Cline

Writers:
Harry Spalding

Director:
Vincent McEveety

Stars:
Vic Morrow, Jeff East, Tom Simcox, Jacqueline Scott

Broadcast:
Mar 13, 1977, NBC

Length:
92 min

Video:
1990s (UK)

The Track of the African Bongo (1977)

The Wonderful World of Disney

Director:
Frank Zuniga

Stars:
Johnny Ngaya, Oliver Litondo, Tony Parkinson, Charles Hayes

Broadcast:
Apr 3, 1977 (Part 1), Apr 10, 1977 (Part 2), NBC

Length:
2 x 50 min

The Bluegrass Special (1977)

The Wonderful World of Disney

Writers:
Sheldon Stark (screenplay), James Algar (story)

Director:
Andrew V. McLaglen

Stars:
William Windom, Celeste Holm, Devon Ericson, Davy Jones

Broadcast:
May 22, 1977, NBC

Length:
48 min

Video:
1986 The Wonderful World of Disney: The Bluegrass Special

DVD:
2006 Disney Movie Club Exclusive

Halloween Hall o' Fame (1977)

The Wonderful World of Disney

Includes:

Trick or Treat (1952), *Pluto's Judgement Day* (1935), *The Legend of Sleepy Hollow* (1949)

Director:

Arthur J. Vitarelli

Stars:

Jonathan Winters

Broadcast:

Oct 30, 1977, NBC

Length:

50 min

The Mouseketeers at Walt Disney World (1977)

The Wonderful World of Disney

Director:

John Tracy

Stars:

Jo Anne Worley, Ronnie Schell, Dennis Underwood

Broadcast:

Nov 20, 1977, NBC

Length:

90 min

Three on the Run (1978)

The Wonderful World of Disney

Writers:

Eric Freiwald, Robert Schaefer

Director:

William Beaudine, Jr.

Stars:

Denver Pyle, Davey Davison, Brett McGuire, Donald Williams

Broadcast:

Jan 8, 1978, NBC

Length:

50 min

Video:

1990s *The Wonderful World of Disney: Three on the Run*

Journey to the Valley of the Emu (1978)

The Wonderful World of Disney

Director:
Roy Edward Disney

Stars:
Victor Palmer

Broadcast:
Jan 22, 1978, NBC

Length:
50 min

The Million Dollar Dixie Deliverance (1978)

The Wonderful World of Disney

Writers:
Lawrence Montaigne

Director:
Russ Mayberry

Stars:
Brock Peters, Christian Juttner, Chip Courtland, Kyle Richards

Broadcast:
Feb 5, 1978, NBC

Length:
90 min

Video:
1990s (UK)

Race for Survival (1978)

The Wonderful World of Disney

Writers:
Jack Couffer

Director:
Jack Couffer

Stars:
Bosco Hogan, Peter Lukoye, Saeed Jaffrey, Dick Thomsett

Broadcast:
Mar 5, 1978, NBC

Length:
50 min

Video:
1990s *The Wonderful World of Disney: Three on the Run*

Trail of Danger (1978)
The Wonderful World of Disney
Director:
Andrew V. McLaglen
Stars:
Larry Wilcox, Jim Davis, Robert Donner, David Ireland
Broadcast:
Mar 12, 1978 (Part 1), Mar 19, 1978 (Part 2), NBC
Length:
2 x 50 min

Child of Glass (1978)
The Wonderful World of Disney
Source:
The Ghost Belonged to Me (1975) Richard Peck
Writers:
Jim Lawrence
Director:
John Erman
Stars:
Barbara Barrie, Biff McGuire, Anthony Zerbe, Nina Foch
Broadcast:
May 14, 1978, NBC
Length:
94 min
Video:
1987
DVD:
2011 Generations Collection

The Young Runaways (1978)
The Wonderful World of Disney
Writers:
Sy Gomberg
Director:
Russ Mayberry

Stars:
Gary Collins, Anne Francis, Sharon Farrell, Robert Webber

Broadcast:
May 28, 1978, NBC

Length:
90 min

Mickey's 50 (1978)

The Wonderful World of Disney

Writers:
Nick Bennion, Phil May

Director:
Phil May

Broadcast:
Nov 19, 1978, NBC

Length:
90 min

Christmas at Walt Disney World (1978)

The Wonderful World of Disney

AKA:
Happy Holidays at Walt Disney World

Writers:
Danny Simon, Doug Beckwith, Avery Schreiber, Steve Binder, Robert Shields

Director:
Steve Binder

Broadcast:
Dec 10, 1978, NBC

Length:
50 min

Donovan's Kid (1979)

The Wonderful World of Disney

Writers:
Peter S. Fischer (story), Harry Spalding (screenplay)

Director:
Bernard McEveety

Stars:
Darren McGavin, Mickey Rooney, Shelley Fabares, Katy Kurtzman

Broadcast:
Jan 7, 1979 (Part 1), Jan 14, 1979 (Part 2), NBC

Length:
2 x 50 min

Shadow of Fear (1979)

The Wonderful World of Disney

Writers:
Gerry Day

Director:
Noel Nosseck

Stars:
Ike Eisenmann, John Anderson, Peter Haskell, Joyce Van Patten

Broadcast:
Jan 28, 1979 (Part 1), Feb 4, 1979 (Part 2), NBC

Length:
2 x 50 min

The Omega Connection (1979)

The Wonderful World of Disney

AKA:
The London Connection (theatrical)

Writers:
Joshua Brand, Martha Coolidge (story), Gail Morgan Hickman, David
E. Boston (screenplay)

Director:
Robert Clouse

Stars:
Jeffrey Byron, Larry Cedar, Roy Kinnear, Lee Montague

Broadcast:
Mar 18, 1979, NBC

Length:
90 min

Movies:
1979 (Europe)

Born to Run (1979)

The Wonderful World of Disney

AKA:
Harness Fever (Australia)

Source:
The Boyds of Black River (1953) Walter D. Edmonds

Writers:
Ed Jurist

Director:
Don Chaffey

Stars:
Tom Farley, Robert Bettles, Andrew McFarlane, Mary Ward

Broadcast:
Mar 25, 1979 (Part 1), Apr 1, 1979 (Part 2), NBC

Length:
87 min (feature), 2 x 50 min (episodes)

Movies:
1977 (Australia/UK)

Video:
1987

The Sky Trap (1979)

The Wonderful World of Disney

Source:
The Sky Trap (1975) D.S. Halacy Jr.

Writers:
Jim Lawrence

Director:
Jerome Courtland

Stars:
Jim Hutton, Marc McClure, Patricia Crowley, Kitty Ruth

Broadcast:
May 13, 1979, NBC

Length:
91 min

Video:
1990s (UK)

Baseball Fever (1979)

Disney's Wonderful World

Includes:

How to Play Baseball (1942), *Casey at the Bat* (1946), *Goofy Gymnastics* (1949), *Slide Donald Slide* (1949), *Lion Down* (1951), *Tomorrow We Diet!* (1951), *Casey Bats Again* (1954)

Directors:

Jack Hannah, Jack Kinney

Broadcast:

Oct 14, 1979, NBC

Length:

50 min

Major Effects (1979)

Disney's Wonderful World

Source:

Behind the scenes of *The Black Hole* (1979)

Writers:

Nicholas Harvey Bennion

Director:

Nicholas Harvey Bennion

Stars:

Joseph Bottoms

Broadcast:

Dec 16, 1979, NBC

Length:

50 min

PART SIX

1980–1984

Donald's Valentine's Day Salute (1980)

Disney's Wonderful World

Includes:
Once Upon a Wintertime (1948), *Donald's Double Trouble* (1946), *Mickey's Delayed Date* (1947), *Wonder Dog* (1950), *Frank Duck Brings 'em Back Alive* (1946)

Broadcast:
Feb 10, 1980, NBC

Length:
50 min

Kraft Salutes Disneyland's 25th Anniversary (1980)

AKA:
Disneyland's 25, Anniversary Show (rerun on *Disney's Wonderful World*)

Writers:
Marty Farrell, Buz Kohan

Director:
Dwight Hemion

Broadcast:
Mar 6, 1980, CBS

Length:
50 min

The Kids Who Knew Too Much (1980)

Disney's Wonderful World

Source:
The Whisper in the Gloom (1954) Nicholas Blake

Writers:
David E. Boston, Gail Morgan Hickman

Director:
Robert Clouse

Stars:
Sharon Gless, Larry Cedar, Rad Daly, Dana Hill

Broadcast:
Mar 9, 1980, NBC

Length:
90 min

Video:
1990s (UK)

Disney's Oscar Winners (1980)

Disney's Wonderful World

Source:
Various Disney shorts and features

Writers:
William Reid

Director:
William Reid

Broadcast:
Apr 13, 1980, NBC

Length:
50 min

The Sultan and the Rock Star (1980)

Disney's Wonderful World

AKA:
The Hunter and the Rock Star

Source:
Sandy and the Rock Star (1979) Walt Morey

Writers:
Steve Hays

Director:
Ed Abroms

Stars:
Timothy Hutton, Ken Swofford, Bruce Glover, Ned Romero

Broadcast:
Apr 20, 1980, NBC

Length:
47 min

Video:
1990s *The Wonderful World of Disney: Dad, Can I Borrow the Car?*

DVD:
2012 Disney Movie Club Exclusive

Digital:
iTunes

The Secret of Lost Valley (1980)

Disney's Wonderful World

Writers:
David Irving (story), Paul Golding (screenplay)

Director:
Vic Morrow

Stars:
Gary Collins, Mary Ann Mobley, Brad Savage, Eddie Marquez

Broadcast:
Apr 27, 1980 (Part 1), May 4, 1980 (Part 2), NBC

Length:
2 x 50 min

Lefty (1980)

AKA:
Lefty: The Carol Johnston Story

Source:
Life of disabled gymnast Carol Johnston (1958+)

Writers:
Gina Rester

Director:
James E. Thompson

Broadcast:
Oct 22, 1980, NBC

Length:
50 min

Shorts:
The Truly Exceptional: Carol Johnston (1979) Original theatrical short, 1981 (International)

The Mouseketeer Reunion (1980)

Disney's Wonderful World

Director:
Tom Trbovich

Broadcast:
Nov 23, 1980, NBC

Length:
50 min

The Ghosts of Buxley Hall (1980-1981)

Disney's Wonderful World

Writers:
Sy Gomberg (story/screenplay), Rick Mittleman (screenplay)

Director:
Bruce Bilson

Stars:
Dick O'Neill, Victor French, Louise Latham, Monte Markham

Broadcast:
Dec 21, 1980 (Part 1), Jan 4, 1981 (Part 2), NBC

Length:
95 min (feature), 2 x 50 min (episodes)

Video:
1990s (UK)

DVD:
2012 Disney Movie Club Exclusive

Digital:
Amazon, iTunes, Vudu

Disney Animation: The Illusion of Life (1981)

Disney's Wonderful World

Source:
- *Disney Animation: The Illusion of Life* (1981) Frank Thomas, Ollie Johnston
- Behind the scenes of *The Fox and the Hound* (1981)

Writers:
Bob King, Phil May (story), William Reid (narration)
Director:
William Reid
Broadcast:
Apr 26, 1981, NBC
Length:
50 min
Video:
1986 *The Wonderful World of Disney: An Adventure in Color including Donald in Mathmagic Land*

The Cherokee Trail (1981)

Walt Disney
Source:
The Cherokee Trail (1982) Louis L'Amour
Writers:
Kieth Merrill, Michael Terrance
Director:
Kieth Merrill
Stars:
Cindy Pickett, Mary Larkin, Timothy Scott, David Hayward
Broadcast:
Nov 28, 1981, CBS
Length:
50 min
TV Series:
Five Mile Creek (Disney Channel, 1983-1985) x 39 episodes, Spin-off [Collection: *The Complete First Season* DVD (2005)]

Walt Disney: One Man's Dream (1981)

Walt Disney
Source:
Life of Walt Disney
Writers:
Stan Hart, John McGreevey, Mitzie Welch
Director:
Dwight Hemion

Broadcast:
Dec 12, 1981, CBS

Length:
90 min

Tales of the Apple Dumpling Gang (1982)

Walt Disney

Source:
Remake of *The Apple Dumpling Gang* (1975)

Director:
E.W. Swackhamer

Stars:
John Bennett Perry, Sandra Kearns, Ed Begley, Jr., Henry Jones

Broadcast:
Jan 16, 1982, CBS

Length:
50 min

TV Series:
Gun Shy (CBS, 1983) x 6 episodes, Spin-off

Beyond Witch Mountain (1982)

Walt Disney

Source:
Sequel to *Escape to Witch Mountain* (1975)

Writers:
Robert Malcolm Young (story/screenplay), B.W. Sandefur

Director:
Robert Day

Stars:
Eddie Albert, Tracey Gold, Andy Freeman, Efrem Zimbalist, Jr.

Broadcast:
Feb 20, 1982, CBS

Length:
48 min

DVD:
2012 Generations Collection

Herbie, the Love Bug (1982)

Source:
Spin-off of *The Love Bug* (1968)

Episodes:
[1]Herbie, the Matchmaker, [2]Herbie to the Rescue, [3]My House Is Your House, [4]Herbie, the Best Man, [5]Calling Doctor Herbie

Writers:
Arthur Alsberg[1,2,4,5], Don Nelson[1,2,4,5], Don Tait[3]

Directors:
Charles S. Dubin[1], Vincent McEveety[2,4], Bill Bixby[3,5]

Stars:
Dean Jones, Patricia Hardy, Richard Paul, Claudia Wells

Broadcast:
Mar 17—Apr 14, 1982, CBS

Length:
5 x 45 min

The Adventures of Pollyanna (1982)

Walt Disney

Source:

- *Pollyanna* (1913) Eleanor H. Porter
- Spin-off of *Pollyanna* (1960)

Writers:
Ann Beckett

Director:
Robert Day

Stars:
Shirley Jones, Patsy Kensit, Edward Winter, Beverly Archer

Broadcast:
Apr 10, 1982, CBS

Length:
50 min

EPCOT Center: The Opening Celebration (1982)

Walt Disney

Source:
Behind the scenes at Walt Disney World

Writers:
Buz Kohan

Director:
Dwight Hemion

Broadcast:
Oct 23, 1982, CBS

Length:
50 min

Disney's Halloween Treat (1982)

Walt Disney

Source:
Various animated shorts and features

Broadcast:
Oct 30, 1982, CBS

Length:
47 min

Video:
1984

A Disney Christmas Gift (1982)

Walt Disney

Source:
Various animated shorts and features

Broadcast:
Dec 4, 1982, CBS

Length:
47 min

Video:
1984, 1985, 1996

Laserdisc:
1990

Gun Shy (1983)

Source:
Spin-off of *The Apple Dumpling Gang* (1975)

Episodes:
[1]Western Velvet, [2]Pardon Me Boy, Is That the Quake City Choo Choo?,
[3]What Do You Mean "We", Amigo?, [4]You Gotta Know When to Hold

'Em, [5]Reading, Writing, and Robbing, [6]Mail Order Mommy

Stars:

Barry Van Dyke, Tim Thomerson, Keith Mitchell, Adam Rich

Broadcast:

Mar 25—Apr 19, 1983, CBS

Length:

6 x 30 min

Small & Frye (1983)

Episodes:

[1]Fiddler on the Hoof, [2]Endangered Detectives, [3]The Case of the Street of Silence, [4]Small & Frye, [5]Schlocky Too, [6]The Case of the Concerned Husband

Writers:

Nick Arnold[1,3,5,6], Leonard Ripps[2], Ron Friedman[4], George Schenck[4]

Directors:

Leslie H. Martinson[1], Edward H. Feldman[2], James Sheldon[3], Charles S. Dubin[4], John Bowab[5], Mel Ferber[6]

Stars:

Darren McGavin, Jack Blessing, Debbie Zipp, Bill Daily

Broadcast:

Mar 7—Jun 15, 1983, CBS

Length:

6 x 30 min

Zorro and Son (1983)

Source:

Spin-off of *Zorro* (1957-1959) TV series

Episodes:

[1]Zorro and Son, [2]Beauty and the Mask, [3]A Fistful of Pesos, [4]Wash Day, [5]The Butcher of Barcelona

Writers:

Eric Cohen[1-5], Nick Arnold[2-5]

Directors:

Peter Baldwin[1,4], Gabrielle Beaumont[2,5], Alan Myerson[3]

Stars:

Henry Darrow, Paul Regina, Bill Dana, Gregory Sierra

Broadcast:

Apr 6—Jun 1, 1983, CBS

Length:
5 x 30 min

The Whale's Tooth (1983)

Director:
Roy Edward Disney

Broadcast:
Oct 22, 1983, Canada

Tiger Town (1983)

Disney Channel Premiere Film

Writers:
Alan Shapiro, Bobby Fine

Director:
Alan Shapiro

Stars:
Justin Henry, Roy Scheider, Ron McClarty, Bethany Carpenter

Broadcast:
Oct 9, 1983, Disney Channel

Length:
76 min

Movies:
1984 (Detroit, US) Limited

Laserdisc:
1987 (Japan)

Video:
1987

Gone are the Dayes (1984)

Disney Channel Premiere Film

Writers:
Jim Blecher, William Bleich

Director:
Gabrielle Beaumont

Stars:
Harvey Korman, Robert Hogan, Susan Anspach, David Glasser

Broadcast:
May 6, 1984, Disney Channel

Length:
90 min

Video:
1984

Love Leads the Way (1984)

Disney Channel Premiere Film

AKA:
Love Leads the Way: A True Story

Writers:
Henry Denker, Jimmy Hawkins

Director:
Delbert Mann

Stars:
Timothy Bottoms, Eva Marie Saint, Ralph Bellamy, Ernest Borgnine

Broadcast:
Oct 7, 1984, Disney Channel

Length:
99 min

Video:
1985

PART SEVEN

1985–1989

Black Arrow (1985)
Disney Channel Premiere Film

Source:
The Black Arrow: A Tale of the Two Roses (1888) Robert Louis Stevenson

Writers:
David Pursall, Harry Alan Towers (aka Peter Welbeck)

Director:
John Hough

Stars:
Oliver Reed, Fernando Rey, Benedict Taylor, Stephan Chase

Broadcast:
Jan 6, 1985, Disney Channel

Length:
93 min

Comic Strips:
Black Arrow (TCT, Jan 6—Mar 31, 1985)

Video:
1985

Lots of Luck (1985)
Disney Channel Premiere Film

Writers:
Deborah Cavanaugh, Eric Loeb

Director:
Peter Baldwin

Stars:
Martin Mull, Annette Funicello, Fred Willard, Polly Holliday

Broadcast:
Feb 3, 1985, Disney Channel

Length:
88 min

Video:
1986

Wildside (1985)

Episodes:
[1]Well Known Secret, [2]Delinquency in a Miner, [3]The Crimea of the Century, [4]Don't Keep the Home Fires Burning, [5]Buffalo Who?, [6]Until the Fat Lady Sings

Writers:
Tom Greene[1], Jonathan Torp[2], Steve Johnson[3], William Whitehead[4], Walter Brough[5]

Directors:
Richard C. Sarafian[1,3,5], Harvey S. Laidman[2,4,6]

Stars:
Howard Rollins, Williams Smith, J. Eddie Peck, John DiAquino

Broadcast:
Mar 21—Apr 25, 1985, ABC

Length:
6 x 48 min

Video:
1980s

The Undergrads (1985)

Disney Channel Premiere Film

Writers:
Michael Weisman (story), Paul W. Shapiro (story/screenplay)

Director:
Steven H. Stern

Stars:
Art Carney, Chris Makepeace, Len Birman, Lesleh Donaldson

Broadcast:
May 5, 1985, Disney Channel

Length:
103 min

Video:
1987

The Blue Yonder (1985)

Disney Channel Premiere Film

AKA:
Time Flyer (rerun on *The Disney Sunday Movie*)

Writers:
Mark Rosman

Director:
Mark Rosman

Stars:
Peter Coyote, Huckleberry Fox, Art Carney

Broadcast:
Nov 17, 1985, Disney Channel

Length:
92 min

Video:
1986

Help Wanted: Kids (1986)

The Disney Sunday Movie

Writers:
Henry Stern (story), Stephen Black (story/screenplay)

Director:
David Greenwalt

Stars:
Cindy Williams, Bill Hudson, Chad Allen, Hillary Wolf

Broadcast:
Feb 2, 1986, ABC

Length:
100 min

TV Series:
Just Like Family (Disney Channel, 1989) Spin-off

The Last Electric Knight (1986)

The Disney Sunday Movie

Writers:
Dan Gordon

Director:
James Fargo

Stars:
Ernie Reyes, Gil Gerard, Keye Luke, Nancy Stafford

Broadcast:
Feb 16, 1986, ABC

Length:
45 min

TV Series:
Sidekicks (ABC, 1986-1987) x 23 episodes, spin-off

2½ Dads (1986)

The Disney Sunday Movie

Writers:
Gordon Fair

Director:
Tony Bill

Stars:
George Dzundza, Lenore Kasdorf, Marissa Mendenhall, Richard Young

Broadcast:
Feb 16, 1986, ABC

Length:
45 min

The Girl Who Spelled Freedom (1986)

The Disney Sunday Movie

Writers:
Christopher Knopf, David A. Simons

Director:
Simon Wincer

Stars:
Wayne Rogers, Mary Kay Place, Jade Chinn, Kieu Chinh

Broadcast:
Feb 23, 1986, ABC

Length:
90 min

Video:
1987

The Richest Cat in the World (1986)

The Disney Sunday Movie

Writers:
Les Alexander, Steve Ditlea (story), Alfa-Betty Olsen, Marshall Efron
(screenplay)

Director:
Greg Beeman

Stars:
Ramon Bieri, Steve Kampmann, Caroline McWilliams, Steve Vinovich

Broadcast:
Mar 9, 1986, ABC

Length:
87 min

DVD:
2012 Generations Collection

Disney Goes to the Oscars (1986)

The Disney Sunday Movie

AKA:
Disney Goes to the Academy Awards

Source:
Various Disney shorts and features

Writers:
Elayne Boosler, Sam Serlin, Andrew Solt

Director:
Andrew Solt

Broadcast:
Mar 23, 1986, ABC

Length:
90 min

I-Man (1986)

The Disney Sunday Movie

Writers:
Howard Friedlander, Ken Peragine

Director:
Corey Allen

Stars:
Scott Bakula, Ellen Bry, Joey Cramer, John Bloom

Broadcast:
Apr 6, 1986, ABC

Length:
93 min

DVD:
2004 (UK)

A Fighting Choice (1986)

The Disney Sunday Movie

Writers:
Craig Buck

Director:
Ferdinand Fairfax

Stars:
Beau Bridges, Karen Valentine, Patrick Dempsey, Lawrence Pressman

Broadcast:
Apr 13, 1986, ABC

Length:
100 min

Mr. Boogedy (1986)

The Disney Sunday Movie

Writers:
Michael Janover

Director:
Oz Scott

Stars:
Richard Masur, Mimi Kennedy, Benjamin Gregory, David Faustino

Broadcast:
Apr 20, 1986, ABC

Length:
45 min

TV Movie:
Bridge of Boogedy (TV, 1987) Sequel

Laserdisc:
1987 (Japan)

DVD:
2015 Disney Movie Club Exclusive / 2-Movie Collection

Digital:
Amazon, iTunes, Vudu

Young Again (1986)
The Disney Sunday Movie
Writers:
David Steven Simon (story), Barbara Hall (screenplay)
Director:
Steven Hilliard Stern
Stars:
Lindsay Wagner, Jack Gilford, Keanu Reeves, Robert Urich
Broadcast:
May 11, 1986, ABC
Length:
90 min

The Deacon Street Deer (1986)
The Disney Sunday Movie
Writers:
James Mangold
Director:
Jackie Cooper
Stars:
Bumper Robinson, Eve Glazier, Mario Lopez, Sean De Veritch
Broadcast:
May 18, 1986, ABC
Length:
46 min

Fuzzbucket (1986)
The Disney Sunday Movie
Writers:
Mick Garris
Director:
Mick Garris
Stars:
Chris Hebert, Phil Fondacaro, Joe Regalbuto, Wendy Phillips
Broadcast:
May 18, 1986, ABC

Length:
46 min
DVD:
2011 Generations Collection
Digital:
Amazon, iTunes, Vudu

Casebusters (1986)

The Disney Sunday Movie

Writers:
George Arthur Bloom, Donald Paul Roos
Director:
Wes Craven
Stars:
Noah Hathaway, Virginia Keehne, Pat Hingle, Gary Riley
Broadcast:
May 25, 1986, ABC
Length:
47 min
Digital:
Amazon, iTunes, Vudu

My Town (1986)

The Disney Sunday Movie

Writers:
Gil Grant
Director:
Gwen Arner
Stars:
Glenn Ford, Meredith Salenger, Mary Jackson, Parker Jacobs
Broadcast:
May 25, 1986, ABC
Length:
46 min
Digital:
iTunes, Vudu

The Parent Trap II (1986)

Disney Channel Premiere Film

Source:
Sequel to *The Parent Trap* (1961)

Writers:
Stuart Krieger

Director:
Ron Mawell

Stars:
Hayley Mills, Tom Skerritt, Carrie Kei Heim, Bridgette Andersen

Broadcast:
Jul 26, 1986, Disney Channel

Length:
81 min

TV Movies:
- *Parent Trap III* (1989)
- *Parent Trap: Hawaiian Honeymoon* (1989)

DVD:
2005 2-Movie Collection

Hero in the Family (1986)

The Disney Sunday Movie

Writers:
John Drimmer, Geoffrey Loftus

Director:
Mel Damski

Stars:
Christopher Collet, Cliff De Young, Annabeth Gish, Darleen Carr

Broadcast:
Sep 28, 1986, ABC

Length:
90 min

Little Spies (1986)

The Disney Sunday Movie

Writers:
John Greg Pain (story), Stephen Bonds, Stephen Greenfield (story/screenplay)

Director:
Greg Beeman

Stars:
Mickey Rooney, Peter Smith, Robert Costanzo, Candace Cameron

Broadcast:
Oct 5, 1986, ABC

Length:
90 min

Spot Marks the X (1986)

Disney Channel Premiere Film

Writers:
Michael Jenning

Director:
Mark Rosman

Stars:
Barret Oliver, Geoffrey Lewis, Natalie Gregory, David Huddleston

Broadcast:
Oct 18, 1986, Disney Channel

Length:
90 min

The B.R.A.T. Patrol (1986)

The Disney Sunday Movie

Writers:
Chris Carter, Michael Patrick Goodman

Director:
Mollie Miller

Stars:
Sean Astin, Tim Thomerson, Jason Pressman, Joe Wright

Broadcast:
Oct 26, 1986, ABC

Length:
91 min

Digital:
Amazon

Ask Max (1986)

The Disney Sunday Movie

Director:
Vincent McEveety

Stars:
Jeff B. Cogen, Ray Walston, Cassie Yates, Gino DeMauro

Broadcast:
Nov 2, 1986, ABC

Length:
45 min

Walt Disney World's 15th Birthday Celebration (1986)

The Disney Sunday Movie

AKA:
Walt Disney World's 15th Anniversary Celebration

Writers:
Bob Arnott, Jeffrey Barron, David Forman, Ken Welch, Mitzie Welch

Director:
Marty Pasetta

Broadcast:
Nov 9, 1986, ABC

Length:
80 min

Down the Long Hills (1986)

Disney Channel Premiere Film

AKA:
Louis L'Amour's Down the Long Hills

Source:
Down the Long Hills (1968) Louis L'Amour

Writers:
Jon Povare, Ruth Povare

Director:
Burt Kennedy

Stars:
Bruce Boxleitner, Thomas Wilson Brown, Lisa MacFarlane, Jack Elam

Broadcast:
Nov 15, 1986, Disney Channel
Length:
89 min

The Leftovers (1986)

The Disney Sunday Movie

Writers:
Steve Slavkin (story), Gen LeRoy (story/screenplay)
Director:
Paul Schneider
Stars:
John Denver, Cindy Williams, George Wyner, Pamela Segal
Broadcast:
Nov 16, 1986, ABC
Length:
94 min
DVD:
2012 Generations Collection

The Thanksgiving Promise (1986)

The Disney Sunday Movie

Source:
Chester, I Love You (1983) Brenton Yorgason, Blaine Yorgason
Writers:
Blaine Yorgason, Peter N. Johnson, Glenn L. Anderson, Craig Holyoak
Director:
Beau Bridges
Stars:
Lloyd Bridges, Beau Bridges, Jordan Bridges, Millie Perkins
Broadcast:
Nov 23, 1986, ABC
Length:
90 min
Soundtrack:
2013 Intrada (CD)

Disney's Fluppy Dogs (1986)

Writers:

Haskell Barkin, Bruce Talkington

Director:

Fred Wolf

Voices:

Marshall Efron, Carl Steven, Clyde Morrow, Hal Smith

Broadcast:

Nov 27, 1986, ABC

Length:

45 min

Sunday Drive (1986)

The Disney Sunday Movie

Writers:

Larry Brand

Director:

Mark Cullingham

Stars:

Tony Randall, Ted Wass, Carrie Fisher, Audra Lindley

Broadcast:

Nov 30, 1986, ABC

Length:

90 min

The Christmas Star (1986)

The Disney Sunday Movie

Writers:

Alan Shapiro (story/screenplay), Carol Dysinger (screenplay)

Director:

Alan Shapiro

Stars:

Edward Asner, René Auberjonois, Jim Metzler, Susan Tyrrell

Broadcast:

Dec 14, 1986, ABC

Length:

93 min

DVD:

2004

Digital:
Amazon, iTunes, Vudu

Star Tours (1986)

The Disney Sunday Movie (½ episode)

Source:
Star Tours attraction at Disneyland (1987-2011)

Broadcast:
Dec 28, 1986, ABC

Length:
20 min

Great Moments in Disney Animation (1987)

The Disney Sunday Movie

Source:
Various animated shorts and features

Writers:
Jim Milio, Andrew Solt, Susan F. Walker

Director:
Andrew Solt

Broadcast:
Jan 18, 1987, ABC

Length:
90 min

Double Switch (1987)

The Disney Sunday Movie

Writers:
Pater Noah (story), John McNamara (screenplay)

Director:
David Greenwalt

Stars:
George Newbern, Elisabeth Shue, Michael Des Barres, Mariclare Costello

Broadcast:
Jan 24, 1987, ABC

Length:
92 min

DVD:
2012 Disney Movie Club Exclusive

You Ruined My Life (1987)

The Disney Sunday Movie

Writers:
Robin Swicord

Director:
David Ashwell

Stars:
Soleil Moon Frye, Paul Reiser, Mimi Rogers, Allen Gafield

Broadcast:
Feb 1, 1987, ABC

Length:
100 min

The Liberators (1987)

The Disney Sunday Movie

Writers:
Kenneth Johnson

Director:
Kenneth Johnson

Stars:
Robert Carradine, Larry B. Scott, Cynthia Dale, Bumper Robinson

Broadcast:
Feb 8, 1987, ABC

Length:
90 min

Soundtrack:
2011 Limited Edition (CD)

Strange Companions (1987)

Disney Channel Premiere Film

Director:
Frank Zuniga

Stars:
Doug McClure, Michael Sharrett, Marj Dusay

Broadcast:

- Dec 4, 1983 (Canada)
- Feb 28, 1987, Disney Channel (US)

Length:
92 min

Bigfoot (1987)

The Disney Sunday Movie

Writers:
John Groves

Director:
Danny Huston

Stars:
Colleen Dewhurst, James Sloyan, Gracie Harrison, Joseph Maher

Broadcast:
Mar 8, 1987, ABC

Length:
90 min

Young Harry Houdini (1987)

The Disney Sunday Movie

Source:
Life of Harry Houndini (1874-1926)

Writers:
James Orr, Jim Cruickshank

Director:
James Orr

Stars:
Wil Wheaton, Jeffrey DeMunn, Kerri Green, Barry Corbin

Broadcast:
Mar 15, 1987, ABC

Length:
90 min

Double Agent (1987)

The Disney Sunday Movie

Writers:
Howard Friedlander, Ken Peragine (story/screenplay), Craig W. Van Sickle, Steven Long Mitchell (screenplay)

Director:
Michael Vejar

Stars:
Michael McKean, John Putch, Susan Walden, Christopher Burton

Broadcast:
Mar 29, 1987, ABC

Length:
90 min

Bride of Boogedy (1987)
The Disney Sunday Movie

Source:
Sequel to *Mr. Boogedy* (TVM, 1986)

Writers:
Michael Janover

Director:
Oz Scott

Stars:
Richard Masur, Mimi Kennedy, Tammy Lauren, David Faustino

Broadcast:
Apr 12, 1987, ABC

Length:
92 min

DVD:
2015 2-Movie Collection

Digital:
Amazon, iTunes, Vudu

Anne of Avonlea: The Continuing Story of Anne of Green Gables (1987)
Disney Channel Premiere Film

AKA:
Anne of Green Gables: The Sequel

Source:
- Sequel to *Anne of Green Gables* (TV, 1985) Non-Disney Canadian mini-series
- *Anne of Avonlea* (1909), *Anne of the Island* (1915) & *Anne of Windy Poplars* (1936) L.M. Montgomery

Writers:
Kevin Sullivan

Director:
Kevin Sullivan

Stars:
Megan Follows, Colleen Dewhurst, Dame Wendy Hiller, Frank Converse

Broadcast:
May 19, 1987—Jun 9, 1987, Disney Channel

Length:
232 min (feature), 4 x 60 min (episodes)

TV Mini-series:

- *Anne of Green Gables: The Continuing Story* (2000) Non-Disney Canadian sequel
- *Anne of Green Gables: A New Beginning* (2008) Non-Disney Canadian sequel

Laserdisc:
1994

Video:
1995

DVD:
2004 Sullivan Entertainment, 2005 Anne of Green Gables: The Collection

Soundtrack:
1997 (CD, Canada)

Not Quite Human (1987)

Disney Channel Premiere Film

Source:
Not Quite Human 1-6 (1985-1986) Seth McEvoy

Writers:
Alan Ormsby

Director:
Steven H. Stern

Stars:
Jay Underwood, Alan Thicke, Joe Bologna, Robyn Lively

Broadcast:
Jun 19, 1987, Disney Channel

Length:
91 min
TV Movies:
- *Not Quite Human II* (1989) Sequel
- *Still Not Quite Human* (1992) Sequel

Video:
1993

The Return of the Shaggy Dog (1987)

The Disney Sunday Movie
Source:
Sequel to *The Shaggy Dog* (1959)
Writers:
Paul Haggis, Diane Wilk
Director:
Stuart Gillard
Stars:
Gary Kroeger, Todd Waring, Michelle Little, Cindy Morgan
Broadcast:
Nov 1, 1987, ABC
Length:
91 min

Student Exchange (1987)

The Disney Sunday Movie
Writers:
Debra Frankel (story), William Davies, William Osborne (screenplay)
Director:
Mollie Miller
Stars:
Viveka Davis, Todd Field, Mitchell Anderson, Heather Graham
Broadcast:
Nov 29, 1987 (Part 1), Dec 6, 1987 (Part 2), ABC
Length:
88 min (feature), 2 x 45 min (episodes)
DVD:
2011 Generations Collection

The Christmas Visitor (1987)

Disney Channel Premiere Film

AKA:

Bushfire Moon, Miracle Down Under

Writers:

Jeff Peck

Director:

George Miller

Stars:

Dee Wallace Stone, John Waters, Nadine Garner, Andrew Ferguson

Broadcast:

Dec 5, 1987, Disney Channel

Length:

106 min

Video:

1987

Waco & Rhinehart (1987)

AKA:

U.S. Marshals: Waco & Rhinehart

Writers:

Lee David Zlotoff

Director:

Christian I. Nyby II

Stars:

Charles C. Hill, Justin Deas, Bill Hootkins, Bob Tzudiker

Broadcast:

Mar 27, 1987, ABC

Length:

90 min

DuckTales: Treasure of the Golden Suns (1987)

Source:

DuckTales (TV series, 1987-1992) Pilot movie

Episodes:

[1]Don't Give Up the Ship, [2]Wronguay in Ronguay, [3]Three Ducks of the Condor, [4]Cold Duck, [5]Too Much of a Gold Thing

Writers:

Jymn Magon, Bruce Talkington, Mark Zaslove

Directors:
Alan Zaslove[1,3,5], Steve Clark[2], Terence Harrison[4]

Broadcast:
Sep 18, 1987, ABC

Length:
90 min

Movies:
DuckTales the Movie: Treasure of the Lost Lamp (1990)

TV Movies:
- *DuckTales: Time is Money* (1988) Syndication
- *Super DuckTales* (1989) NBC, The Magical World of Disney
- *A DuckTales Valentine* (1990) NBC, The Magical World of Disney

TV Series:
- *DuckTales* (1987-1992) Syndication, 100 episodes [Collection Vols 1-4 DVD (2005-2007, 2013, 2018) 100 episodes / iTunes Vol 1-6 (2016) 100 episodes]
- *DuckTales* (2017+) Disney XD

Video Games:
- *DuckTales* (1989) NES, GB
- *Disney's DuckTales: The Quest for Gold* (1989) Amiga, AII, AST, C64, PC
- *DuckTales 2* (1993) NES, GB
- *DuckTales: Remastered* (2013) PS3, WU, PC, X360S, X360

DVD:
2006, 2013 *Ducktales: Volume 2* (Individual episodes)

Digital:
iTunes (Individual episodes)

Earth*Star Voyager (1988)

The Disney Sunday Movie

AKA:
Earth Star Voyager

Writers:
Ed Spielman

Director:
James Goldstone

Stars:
Duncan Regehr, Brian McNamara, Julia Montgomery, Jason Michas

Broadcast:
Jan 17, 1988 (Part 1), Jan 24, 1988 (Part 2), ABC
Length:
2 x 90 mins

Rock 'n' Roll Mom (1988)

The Disney Sunday Movie

Writers:
Gen LeRoy
Director:
Michael Schultz
Stars:
Dyan Cannon, Michael Brandon, Telma Hopkins, Nancy Lenehan
Broadcast:
Feb 7, 1988, ABC
Length:
94 min
Video:
1988 (*Rock 'n' Roll Mum*, UK/France)

14 Going on 30 (1988)

The Disney Sunday Movie

Writers:
Richard Jeffries (screenplay), James Orr, Jim Cruickshank (story)
Director:
Paul Schneider
Stars:
Steve Eckholdt, Adam Carl, Gabey Olds, Daphne Ashbrook
Broadcast:
Mar 6, 1988 (Part 1), Mar 13, 1988 (Part 2), ABC
Length:
82 min (feature), 2 x 45 min (episodes)
Video:
1988

Save the Dog! (1988)

Disney Channel Premiere Film

Writers:
John McNamara, Haris Orkin

Director:
Paul Aaron

Stars:
Cindy Williams, Tony Randallm, Katherine Helmond, Tom Poston

Broadcast:
Mar 19, 1988, Disney Channel

Length:
87 min

Splash, Too (1988)

The Disney Sunday Movie

Source:
Sequel to *Splash* (1984, Touchstone)

Writers:
Bruce Franklin Singer

Director:
Greg Antonacci

Stars:
Todd Waring, Amy Yasbeck, Donovan Scott, Rita Taggart

Broadcast:
May 1, 1988 (Part 1), May 8, 1988 (Part 2), ABC

Length:
87 min

Video:
1988 (UK/Australia)

Justin Case (1988)

The Disney Sunday Movie

Includes:
Captain EO Backstage (1988), edited from *The Making of Captain EO* (TV, 1986)

Writers:
Blake Edwards (story/screenplay), Jennifer Edwards (story)

Director:
Blake Edwards

Stars:
George Carlin, Molly Hagan, Timothy Stack, Kevin McClarnon

Broadcast:
May 15, 1988, ABC

Length:
71 min
Video:
1988 (Australia)

Meet the Munceys (1988)

The Disney Sunday Movie

Writers:
Chris Carter
Director:
Noel Black
Stars:
Nana Visitor, Peggy Pope, Carmine Caridi, Dan Gauthier
Broadcast:
May 22, 1988, ABC
Length:
100 min

The Night Train to Kathmandu (1988)

Disney Channel Premiere Film

Writers:
Robert Wiemer, Ian Robert
Director:
Robert Wiemer
Stars:
Pernell Roberts, Eddie Castrodad, Milla Jovovich, Kavi Raz
Broadcast:
Jun 5, 1988, Disney Channel
Length:
102 min
Video:
1988 (Paramount)

Ollie Hopnoodle's Haven of Bliss (1988)

Disney Channel Premiere Film

Source:
Short story in *Wanda Hickey's Night of Golden Memories* (1971) Jean Shepherd

Writers:
Jean Shepherd

Director:
Dick Bartlett

Stars:
James B. Sikking, Dorothy Lyman, Jerry O'Connell, Jason Clarke Adams

Broadcast:
Aug 6, 1988, Disney Channel

Length:
89 min

Video:
1993

A Friendship in Vienna (1988)

Disney Channel Premiere Film

Source:
The Devil in Vienna (1978) Doris Orgel

Writers:
Richard Alfieri

Director:
Arthur Allan Seidelman

Stars:
Ed Asner, Jane Alexander, Stephen Macht, Jenny Lewis

Broadcast:
Aug 27, 1988, Disney Channel

Length:
94 min

Video:
1993

The Magical World of Disney (1988)

The Magical World of Disney

Source:
Introduction to new anthology series

Writers:
Sam Egan, Peter Elbling, Steven Kunes

Director:
Max Fader

Broadcast:
Oct 9, 1988, NBC

Length:
48 min

Disney's All-American Sports Nuts (1988)

The Magical World of Disney

Source:
Clips from various Disney movies and shorts

Writers:
Phil Hahn, Tom Perew

Director:
Chep Dobrin

Broadcast:
Oct 16, 1988, NBC

Length:
90 min

Good Old Boy (1988)

Disney Channel Premiere Film

AKA:
Good Old Boy: A Delta Boyhood, The River Pirates

Source:
Good Old Boy: A Delta Boyhood (1971) Willie Morris

Writers:
Paul W. Cooper

Director:
Tom G. Robertson

Stars:
Richard Farnsworth, Ryan Francis, Gennie James, Doug Emerson

Broadcast:
Nov 11, 1988, Disney Channel

Length:
108 min

Video:
1994 (Vidmark Entertainment)

Mickey's 60th Birthday (1988)

The Magical World of Disney

Source:
Includes clips from various movies and shorts

Writers:
Scott Garen

Director:
Scott Garen, Joie Albrecht

Broadcast:
Nov 13, 1988, NBC

Length:
48 min

Davy Crockett: Rainbow in the Thunder (1988)

The Magical World of Disney

Source:
Davy Crockett #6

Writers:
William Blinn

Director:
Ian Thomas

Stars:
Tim Dunigan, Gary Grubbs, Samantha Eggar, David Hemmings

Broadcast:
Nov 20, 1988, NBC

Length:
90 min

TV Anthology:
- *Davy Crockett: A Natural Man* (1988)
- *Davy Crockett: Guardian Spirit* (1989)
- *Davy Crockett: A Letter to Polly* (1989)
- *Davy Crockett: Warrior's Farewell* (1989)

Video:
1988 (UK/Australia)

The Absent-Minded Professor (1988)

The Magical World of Disney

Source:
- Based on *The Absent-Minded Professor* (1961)
- 'A Situation of Gravity' in *Liberty* (1943) Samuel W. Taylor

Writers:
Richard Chapman, Bill Dial

Director:
Robert Scheerer

Stars:
Harry Anderson, Mary Page Keller, Cory Danziger, David Paymer

Broadcast:
Nov 27, 1988, NBC

Length:
90 min

TV Movie:
The Absent-Minded Professor: Trading Places (1989) Sequel

Goodbye, Miss 4th of July (1988)

Disney Channel Premiere Film

Source:
Miss 4, of July, Goodbye (1986) Christopher G. Janus

Writers:
Kathy McCormick

Director:
George Miller

Stars:
Roxana Zal, Chris Sarandon, Chantal Contouri, Louis Gossett, Jr.

Broadcast:
Dec 3, 1988, Disney Channel

Length:
89 min

Video:
1993

Disneyland's All-Star Comedy Circus (1988)

The Magical World of Disney

Writers:
Jeffrey Barron, Turk Pipkin, Saul Ilson

Director:
Stan Harris

Broadcast:
Dec 11, 1988, NBC

Length:
90 min

Davy Crockett: A Natural Man (1988)

The Magical World of Disney

Source:
Davy Crockett #7

Writers:
William Blinn

Director:
David Hemmings

Stars:
Tim Dunigan, Barry Corbin, Rodger Gibson, Molly Hagan

Broadcast:
Dec 18, 1988, NBC

Length:
65 min

DuckTales: Time is Money (1988)

Source:
Spin-off from *DuckTales* (TV series, 1987-1992)

Episodes:
[1]Making Time, [2]The Duck Who Would Be King, [3]Bubba Trubba, [4]Ducks on the Lam, [5]Ali Bubba's Cave

Writers:
Bruce Talkington, Jymn Magon, Bruce Coville[2], Len Uhley[2,3,4,5], Doug Hutchinson[5]

Director:
Bob Hathcock[1,2,3], Terence Harrison[2], Jamie Mitchell[3], James T. Walker[3,4,5]

Broadcast:
Nov 25, 1988, syndication

Length:
90 min

DVD:
2007/2013 *DuckTales: Volume 3* (Individual episodes)

Digital:
Amazon, iTunes (Individual episodes)

Davy Crockett: Guardian Spirit (1989)

The Magical World of Disney

Source:
Davy Crockett #8

Writers:
Deborah Gilliland, Robert Sonntag

Director:
Harry Falk

Stars:
Tm Dunigan, Garry Grubbs, Garry Chalk, Evan Adams

Broadcast:
Jan 13, 1989, NBC

Length:
90 min

Wild Jack (1989)

The Magical World of Disney

Writers:
William Blinn (screenplay)

Director:
Harry Harris, James Quinn

Stars:
John Schneider, Carol Huston, Richard Coca, Jack Kehler

Broadcast:
Jan 15, 1989 (Part 1), Jul 9, 1989 (Part 2), Jul 16, 1989 (Part 3)

Length:
3 x 90 min

Mickey's Happy Valentine Special (1989)

The Magical World of Disney

Source:
Edited from various movies and shorts

Writers:
Joie Albrecht, Scott Garen

Director:
Joie Albrecht, Scott Garen

Broadcast:
Feb 12, 1989, NBC

Length:
90 min

The Absent-Minded Professor: Trading Places (1989)

The Magical World of Disney

Source:
Sequel to *The Absent-Minded Professor* (TV, 1988)

Writers:
Richard Chapman, Bill Dial

Director:
Bob Sweeney

Stars:
Harry Anderson, Mary Page Keller, Ed Begley Jr., James Noble

Broadcast:
Feb 26, 1989, NBC

Length:
90 min

Super DuckTales (1989)

The Magical World of Disney

Source:
Spin-off from *DuckTales* (TV series, 1987-1992)

Episodes:
[1]Liquid Assets, [2]Frozen Assets, [3]Full Metal Duck, [4]The Billionaire Beagle Boys Club, [5]Money to Burn

Writers:
David Weimers, Ken Koonce, Jymn Magon

Director:
James T. Walker

Broadcast:
Mar 26, 1989, NBC

Length:
97 min

DVD:
2007/2013 *DuckTales: Volume 3* (Individual episodes)

Digital:
Amazon, iTunes (Individual episodes)

The Parent Trap III (1989)

The Magical World of Disney

Source:
Second sequel to *The Parent Trap* (1961)

Writers:
Jill Donner (story/screenplay), Deborah Amelon (story)

Director:
Mollie Miller

Stars:
Hayley Mills, Barry Bostwick, Patricia Richardson, Ray Baker

Broadcast:
Apr 9, 1989 (Part 1), Apr 16, 1989 (Part 2), NBC

Length:
86 min

Teen Angel (1989)

The All New Mickey Mouse Club

Stars:
Jason Priestley, Adam Biesk, Renee O'Connor

Broadcast:
Apr 24—May 19, 1989, Disney Channel

Length:
12 x 60 min episodes

TV Serial:
Teen Angel Returns (1989)

Danny, the Champion of the World (1989)

Disney Channel Premiere Film

AKA:
Roald Dahl's Danny the Champion of the World

Source:
Danny, the Champion of the World (1975) Roald Dahl

Writers:
John Goldsmith

Director:
Gavin Miller

Stars:
Jeremy Irons, Robbie Coltrane, Samuel Irons, Cyril Cusack

Broadcast:
Apr 29, 1989, Disney Channel

Length:
99 min

DVD:
2005 UK/Warner Bros.

The Disney-MGM Studios Theme Park Grand Opening (1989)

The Magical World of Disney

Writers:
Lane Sarasohn

Director:
Jeff Margolis

Broadcast:
Apr 30, 1989, NBC

Length:
90 min

Looking for Miracles (1989)

Disney Channel Premiere Film

Source:
Looking for Miracles (1975) A.E. Hotchner

Writers:
Kevin Sullivan, Stuart McLean

Director:
Kevin Sullivan

Stars:
Greg Spottiswood, Patricia Phillips, Zachary Bennett, Joe Flaherty

Broadcast:
Jun 3, 1989, Disney Channel

Length:
103 min

DVD:
2003 (Sullivan Entertainment)

Davy Crockett: A Letter to Polly (1989)
The Magical World of Disney

Source:
Davy Crockett #9

Writers:
Paul Savage

Director:
Harry Falk

Stars:
Tim Dunigan, Aeryk Egan, Garry Chalk, Gary Grubbs

Broadcast:
Jun 11, 1989, NBC

Length:
90 min

Davy Crockett: Warrior's Farewell (1989)
The Magical World of Disney

Source:
Davy Crocket #10

Director:
James J. Quinn

Stars:
Tim Dunigan, Ken Swofford, Clem Fox, Gary Grubbs

Broadcast:
Jun 18, 1989, NBC

Length:
90 min

Great Expectations (1989)

Disney Channel Premiere Film

Source:

Great Expectations (1861) Charles Dickens

Writers:

John Goldsmith

Director:

Kevin Connor

Stars:

John Rhys-Davies, Jean Simmons, Anthony Hopkins, Anthony Calf

Broadcast:

Jul 9—24, 1989, Disney Channel

Length:

308 min

Video:

1989, 1996

Not Quite Human II (1989)

Disney Channel Premiere Film

Source:

- Sequel to *Not Quite Human* (TV Movie, 1987)
- *Not Quite Human* 1-6 (1985-1986) Seth McEvoy

Writers:

Eric Luke

Director:

Eric Luke

Stars:

Jay Underwood, Alan Thicke, Robyn Lively, Katie Barberi

Broadcast:

Sep 23, 1989, Disney Channel

Length:

92 min

Video:

1993

Brand New Life: Above and Beyond Therapy (1989)

The Magical World of Disney

Source:
- Follows *Brand New Life: The Honeymooners* (Non-Disney TV Movie, 1989)
- Brand New Life #2

Writers:
Chris Carter

Stars:
Barbara Eden, Don Murray, Shawnee Smith, Jennie Garth

Broadcast:
Oct 1, 1989, NBC

Length:
60 min

TV Anthology:
- *Brand New Life: I Fought the Law* (1989)
- *Brand New Life: Private School* (1989)
- *Brand New Life: Children of a Legal Mom* (1990)
- *Brand New Life: Even Housekeepers Sing the Blues* (Unaired)

Brand New Life: I Fought the Law (1989)

The Magical World of Disney

Source:
Brand New Life #3

Writers:
Chris Carter

Stars:
Barbara Eden, Don Murray, Shawnee Smith, Jennie Garth

Broadcast:
Oct 15, 1989, NBC

Length:
60 min

Brand New Life: Private School (1989)

The Magical World of Disney

Source:
Brand New Life #4

Writers:
Dori Pierson

Director:
Eric Laneuville

Stars:
Barbara Eden, Don Murray, Shawnee Smith, Jennie Garth

Broadcast:
Oct 22, 1989, NBC

Length:
60 min

Polly (1989)

The Magical World of Disney

Source:
- *Pollyanna* (1913) Eleanor H. Porter
- Remake of *Pollyanna* (1960)

Writers:
William Blinn

Director:
Debbie Allen

Stars:
Keshia Knight Pulliam, Phylicia Rashad, Dorian Harewood, Barbara Montgomery

Broadcast:
Nov 12, 1989, NBC

Length:
93 min

TV Anthology:
Polly: Comin' Home (1990) Sequel

DVD:
2008 Disney Movie Club Exclusive

Soundtrack:
1989 (CD)

The Parent Trap IV: Hawaiian Honeymoon (1989)

The Magical World of Disney

Source:
Third sequel to *The Parent Trap* (1961)

Writers:
John McNamara

Director:
Mollie Miller

Stars:
Hayley Mills, Barry Bostwick, John M. Jackson, Sasha Mitchell

Broadcast:
Nov 19, 1989 (Part 1), Nov 26, 1989 (Part 2), NBC

Length:
100 min

Spooner (1989)

Disney Channel Premiere Film

Writers:
Peter I. Baloff, Dave Wollert

Director:
George Miller

Stars:
Robert Urich, Jane Kaczmarek, Brent Fraser, Paul Gleason

Broadcast:
Dec 2, 1989, Disney Channel

Length:
98 min

A Mother's Courage: The Mary Thomas Story (1989)

The Magical World of Disney

Source:
Biography of basketball star Isiah Thomas (1961-) and his mother

Writers:
Jason Miller

Director:
John Patterson

Stars:
Alfre Woodard, A.J. Johnson, Leon, Garland Spencer

Broadcast:
Dec 3, 1989, NBC (Part 1), Dec 10, 1989, NBC (Part 2)

Length:
87 min

Chip 'n Dale's Rescue Rangers to the Rescue (1989)

AKA:
Rescue Rangers to the Rescue

Source:
Spin-off from *Chip 'n Dale: Rescue Rangers* (TV series, 1988-1990)

Episodes:
To the Rescue: Parts 1-5

Writers:
Jymn Magon[1,2,3,5], Tad Stones[1,2,3,4], Mark Zaslove[1,2,3,5], Kevin Hopps[2,4], Julia Lewald[3]

Directors:
John Kimball, Bob Zamboni, Rick Leon, Jamie Mitchell

Broadcast:
Sep 30, 1989, Syndication

Length:
90 min

Comic Strips:
- *Chip 'n' Dale Rescue Rangers* (#1-19, Jun 1990—Dec 1991)
- *Chip 'n' Dale Rescue Rangers* (#1-8, Dec 2010—Jul 2011) [Collection: *Chip 'n' Dale Rescue Rangers: Slippin' Through the Cracks* (2011)]
- *Chip 'n' Dale Rescue Rangers: Worldwide Rescue* (2011)

Theme Parks:
Gadget's Go Coaster (DL 1993+), (TDL 1996+)

Video Games:
- *Chip 'n Dale Rescue Rangers* (1990) NES
- *Chip 'n Dale Rescue Rangers: The Adventures in Nimnul's Castle* (1990) PC
- *Chip 'n Dale Rescue Rangers 2* (1993) NES

DVD:
2005, 2013 *Chip 'n Dale Rescue Rangers: Volume 1* (Individual episodes)

Digital:
2016 (iTunes) *Chip 'n Dale Rescue Rangers: Volume 2* (Individual episodes)

Teen Angel Returns (1989)

The All New Mickey Mouse Club

Source:
Sequel to *Teen Angel* (1989) TV serial

Stars:
Jason Priestley, Robyn Lively, Scott Reeves, Jennie Garth

Broadcast:
Oct 2—Oct 27, 1989, Disney Channel

Length:
13 x 60 min episodes

The Secret of Lost Creek (1989)

The All New Mickey Mouse Club

Stars:
Shannon Doherty, Scott Bremner, Jody Montana, Dabbs Greer

Broadcast:
Oct 30—Nov 27, 1989, Disney Channel

Length:
5 x 60 min episodes

PART EIGHT

1990–1994

Brand New Life:
Children of a Legal Mom (1990)

The Magical World of Disney

Source:
Brand New Life #5

Writers:
Chris Carter

Director:
Steven Robman

Stars:
Barbara Eden, Don Murray, Shawnee Smith, Jennie Garth

Broadcast:
Jan 7, 1990, NBC

Length:
60 min

Exile (1990)

The Magical World of Disney

Writers:
Jonathan Lemkin, Patrick Hasburgh

Director:
David Greenwalt

Stars:
Chirstopher David Barnes, Corey Feldman, Mike Preston, Michael Stoyanov

Broadcast:
Jan 14, 1990, NBC

Length:
92 min

Lantern Hill (1990)

Disney Channel Premiere Film

Source:
Jane of Lantern Hill (1937) L.M. Montgomery

Writers:
Fiona McHugh, Kevin Sullivan

Director:
Kevin Sullivan

Stars:
Sam Waterston, Mairon Bennett, Colleen Dewhurst, Sarah Polley

Broadcast:
Jan 27, 1990, Disney Channel

Length:
112 min

DVD:
2003 Sullivan Entertainment

Disneyland's 35th Anniversary Celebration (1990)

The Magical World of Disney

Writers:
Joie Albrecht, Daniel Butler, Scott Garen, Joe Guppy, Nancy Harris, Glenn Petach, Bill Prady

Director:
James Burrows, John R. Cherry III, John Landis

Broadcast:
Feb 4, 1990, NBC

Length:
60 min

A DuckTales Valentine (1990)

The Magical World of Disney

AKA:
A DuckTales Valentine (Amour or Less)

Includes:
A Disney Valentine (TV, 1982)

Source:
Spin-off from *DuckTales* (TV series, 1987-1992)
Writers:
Len Uhley
Director:
Mircea Mantta
Broadcast:
Feb 11, 1990, NBC
Length:
22 min
DVD:
2018 *DuckTales: Volume 4*
Digital:
2016 Amazon, iTunes (Vol 6)

Sky High (1990)

The Magical World of Disney
Writers:
Ruben Gordon, Steve Schoenberg
Directors:
James Whitmore Jr. (Part 1), James Fargo (Part 2)
Stars:
Damon Martin, Anthony Rapp, James Whitmore, Traci Lind
Broadcast:
Mar 11, 1990 (Part 1), Aug 26, 1990 (Part 2), NBC
Length:
120 min (Part 1), 60 min (Part 2)

Chips, the War Dog (1990)

Disney Channel Premiere Film
Source:
Based on a true story
Writers:
Sandra Weintraub (story), Michael Pardridge, Janice Hickey (screenplay)
Director:
Ed Kaplan
Stars:
Brandon Douglas, William Devane, Paxton Whitehead, Ellie Cornell

Broadcast:
Mar 24, 1990, Disney Channel

Length:
92 min

Video:
1993

Just Perfect (1990)

The All New Mickey Mouse Club

Stars:
Christopher Daniel Barnes, Jennie Garth, Sean Patrick Flanery

Broadcast:
Apr 9—May 4, 1990, Disney Channel

Length:
? x 60 min episodes

The Muppets at Walt Disney World (1990)

The Magical World of Disney

Writers:
Jerry Juhl

Director:
Peter Harris

Stars:
Charles Grodin, Raven-Symoné

Broadcast:
May 6, 1990, NBC

Length:
60 min

Mother Goose Rock 'n' Rhyme (1990)

Disney Channel Premiere Film

AKA:
Shelley Duvall's Mother Goose Rock 'n' Rhyme

Writers:
Linda Engelsiepen, Hilary Hinkle (story), Mark Curtiss (screenplay)

Director:
Jeff Stein

Stars:
Shelley Duvall, Jean Stapleton, Cyndi Lauper, Debbie Harry

Broadcast:
May 19, 1990, Disney Channel
Length:
96 min
Video:
1998

Back Home (1990)

Disney Channel Premiere Film

Source:
Back Home (1984) Michelle Magorian
Writers:
David Wood
Director:
Piers Haggard
Stars:
Hayley Mills, Hayley Carr, Adam Stevenson, Brenda Bruce
Broadcast:
Jun 7, 1990, Disney Channel
Length:
103 min
Video:
1993

The Little Kidnappers (1990)

Disney Channel Premiere Film

Source:
Remake of *The Little Kidnappers* (United Artists, 1953)
Writers:
Coralee Elliott Testar
Director:
Donald Shebib
Stars:
Charlton Heston, Patricia Gage, Leah Pinsett, Charles Miller
Broadcast:
Aug 17, 1990, Disney Channel
Length:
92 min

Video:
1998 Bonneville Worldwide

DVD:
1990, 2013 10 Movie Adventure Pack: Volume Three, 2015 4-Film Classic Family Collection (all Echo Bridge Entertainment)

Digital:
Amazon, iTunes

Soundtrack:
2017 *The Mark Snow Collection Volume 1: Orchestral* (CD)

TaleSpin: Plunder & Lightning (1990)

AKA:
Disney's TaleSpin: Plunder & Lightning

Source:
Spin-off from *TaleSpin* (TV Series, 1990-1994)

Episodes:
Plunder and Lightning: Parts 1-4

Writers:
Alan Burnett, Len Uhley, Mark Zaslove

Directors:
Larry Latham, Robert Taylor

Broadcast:
Sep 7, 1990, Syndication

Length:
90 min

Comic Book:
TaleSpin (#1-4 & #1-7, 1991)

DVD:
2006, 2013 *TaleSpin: Volume 1* (Individual episodes)

Digital:
iTunes (Individual episodes)

My Life as a Babysitter (1990)

The All New Mickey Mouse Club

Stars:
Jim Calvert, Kelli Williams, Shane Meier, Michele Abrams

Broadcast:
Oct 15—Nov 9, 1990, Disney Channel

Length:
? x 60 min episodes

Back to Hannibal: The Return of Tom Sawyer and Huckleberry Finn (1990)

Disney Channel Premiere Film

Source:
Based on characters created by Mark Twain

Writers:
Roy Johansen

Director:
Paul Krasny

Stars:
Paul Winfield, Raphael Sbarge, Mitchell Anderson, Ned Beatty

Broadcast:
Oct 21, 1990, Disney Channel

Length:
92 min

Laserdisc:
1992

Video:
1997

DVD:
2012 Disney Generations Collection

Polly: Comin' Home! (1990)

Source:
Sequel to *Polly* (TV Anthology, 1989)

Writers:
William Blinn

Director:
Debbie Allen

Stars:
Keshia Knight Pulliam, Phylicia Rashad, Dorian Harewood, Barbara Montgomery

Broadcast:
Nov 18, 1990, NBC

Length:
100 min

DVD:
2008 Disney Movie Club Exclusive

A Mom for Christmas (1990)

Source:
A Mom by Magic (1990) Barbara Dillon

Writers:
Gerald Di Pego

Director:
George Miller

Stars:
Olivia Newton-John, Juliet Sorci, Doug Sheehan, Carmen Argenziano

Broadcast:
Dec 17, 1990, NBC

Length:
96 min

DVD:
2008 Disney Movie Club Exclusive

Bejewelled (1991)

Disney Channel Premiere Film

Source:
Bejewelled Death (1981) Marian Babson

Writers:
Tom J. Astle

Director:
Terry Marcwl

Stars:
Emma Samms, Dirk Benedict, Denis Lawson, Jade Magri

Broadcast:
Jan 20, 1991, Disney Channel

Length:
94 min

Perfect Harmony (1991)

Disney Channel Premiere Film

Writers:
David Obst

Director:
Will Mackenzie

Stars:
Justin Whalin, Eugene Byrd, Darren McGavin, David Faustino

Broadcast:
Mar 31, 1991, Disney Channel

Length:
93 min

Video:
2003

DVD:
2004

The 100 Lives of Black Jack Savage (1991)

Director:
Kim Manners (Pilot movie)

Stars:
Daniel Hugh Kelly, Steven Williams, Steve Hytner, Roma Downey

Broadcast:
Mar 31, 1991, NBC (Pilot movie), Apr 5—May 26, 1991, NBC (Series)

Length:
83 min (Pilot movie), 6 x 42 min episodes (Series)

She Stood Alone (1991)

Writers:
Bruce Franklin Singer

Director:
Jack Gold

Stars:
Mare Winningham, Ben Cross, Robert Desiderio, Daniel Davis

Broadcast:
Apr 15, 1991, NBC

Length:
95 min

Secret Bodyguard (1991)

The All New Mickey Mouse Club

Stars:
Ernie Reyes, Jr., Heather Campbell, Stephen Burton, Johnny Moran

Broadcast:
Sep 9, 1991 - ?, Disney Channel

Mark Twain and Me (1991)

Disney Channel Premiere Film

Source:
Mark Twain and Me (1961) Dorothy Quick

Writers:
Cynthia Whitcomb

Director:
Daniel Petrie

Stars:
Jason Robards, Amy Stewart, Talia Shire, R.H. Thompson

Broadcast:
Nov 22, 1991, Disney Channel

Length:
93 min

Video:
1997

Soundtrack:
1995 *Laurence Rosenthal: Music for Television* (CD, 5 tracks)

In the Nick of Time (1991)

Writers:
Jon S. Denny (story), Rick Podell, Michael Preminger, Maryedith Burrell (screenplay)

Director:
George Miller

Stars:
Lloyd Bridges, Michael Tucker, Alison LaPlaca, Jessica DiCiccio

Broadcast:
Dec 16, 1991, NBC

Length:
89 min

Length:
? x 60 min episodes

Day-O (1992)

AKA:
Dayo

Writers:
Bruce Franklin Singer

Director:
Michael Schultz

Stars:
Delta Burke, Elijah Wood, Carlin Glynn, Charles Shaughnessy

Broadcast:
May 3, 1992, NBC

Length:
90 min

Still Not Quite Human (1992)

Disney Channel Premiere Film

Source:
- Second sequel to *Not Quite Human* (TV Movie, 1987)
- *Not Quite Human* 1-6 (1985-1986) Seth McEvoy

Writers:
Eric Luke

Director:
Eric Luke

Stars:
Jay Underwood, Alan Thicke, Christopher Neame, Betsy Palmer

Broadcast:
May 31, 1992, Disney Channel

Length:
84 min

Video:
1993

The Ernest Green Story (1993)

Disney Channel Premiere Film

Source:
True story of Ernest Green (1941-)

Writers:
Lawrence Roman

Director:
Eric Laneuville

Stars:
Morris Chestnut, CCH Pounder, Gary Grubbs, Tina Lifford

Broadcast:
Jan 17, 1993, Disney Channel

Length:
101 min

Video:
1993

DVD:
2012 Classroom Edition

Spies (1993)

Disney Channel Premiere Film

Writers:
Thomas Hood

Director:
Kevin Connor

Stars:
Shiloh Strong, David Dukes, Cloris Leachman, Eric Paisley

Broadcast:
Mar 7, 1993, Disney Channel

Length:
88 min

Miracle Child (1993)

Source:
Miracle at Clement's Pond (1987) Patricia Pendergraft

Writers:
Gerald Di Pego

Director:
Michael Pressman

Stars:
Crystal Bernard, Cloris Leachman, John Terry, Graham Stack

Broadcast:
Apr 6, 1993, NBC

Length:
100 min

Emerald Cove (1993)
The All New Mickey Mouse Club
Stars:
Tony Lucca, Marc Worden, Ricky Luna, Matt Morris
Broadcast:
Jun 26, 1993 - ?, Disney Channel
Length:
? x 30 min episodes

Heidi (1993)
Disney Channel Premiere Film
Source:
Heidi (1881) Johanna Spyri
Writers:
Jeanne Rosenberg
Director:
Michael Rhodes
Stars:
Jason Robards, Noley Thornton, Jane Seymour, Patricia Neal
Broadcast:
Jul 18, 1993, Disney Channel
Length:
193 min
Video:
1994
DVD:
2005, 2014 (FilmRise)
Digital:
Amazon

One More Mountain (1994)
The Wonderful World of Disney
Source:
Based on a true story
Writers:
John A. Kuri (story/screenplay), Gerald Di Pego (screenplay)

Director:
Dick Lowery

Stars:
Meredith Baxter, Chris Cooper, Larry Drake, Jean Simmons

Broadcast:
Mar 6, 1994, ABC

Length:
90 min

Digital:
Amazon, iTunes, Vudu

On Promised Land (1994)

Disney Channel Premiere Film

Writers:
Ken Sagoes

Director:
Joan Tewkesbury

Stars:
Joan Plowright, Norman D. Golden II, Judith Ivey, Carl Lumbly

Broadcast:
Apr 17, 1994, Disney Channel

Length:
99 min

The Whipping Boy (1994)

Disney Channel Premiere Film

AKA:
Prince Brat and the Whipping Boy

Source:
The Whipping Boy (1986) Sid Fleischman

Writers:
Albert Sidney Fleischman (as Max Brindle)

Director:
Syd Macartney

Stars:
Truan Munro, Nic Knight, George C. Scott, Kevin Conway

Broadcast:
Jul 31, 1994, Disney Channel

Length:
96 min
Video:
1996 (Sony Pictures)
DVD:
2009 (Columbia Pictures)
Digital:
Amazon

The Shaggy Dog (1994)

Source:
Remake of *The Shaggy Dog* (1959)
Writers:
Bill Walsh, Lillie Hayward, Tim Doyle
Director:
Dennis Dugan
Stars:
Scott Weinger, Ed Begley, Jr., Jordan Blake, James Cromwell
Broadcast:
Nov 12, 1994, ABC
Length:
96 min

PART NINE

1995–1999

The Computer Wore Tennis Shoes (1995)

Source:
Remake of *The Computer Wore Tennis Shoes* (1969)

Writers:
Joseph L. McEveety, Ryan Rowe

Director:
Peyton Reed

Stars:
Kirk Cameron, Larry Miller, Jason Bernard, Jeff Maynard

Broadcast:
Feb 18, 1995, ABC

Length:
87 min

The Old Curiosity Shop (1995)

Disney Channel Premiere Film

Source:
The Old Curiosity Shop (1841) Charles Dickens

Writers:
John Goldsmith

Director:
Kevin Connor

Stars:
Peter Ustinov, Tom Courtenay, Sally Walsh, James Fox

Broadcast:
Mar 19—20, 1995, Disney Channel

Length:
188 min

DVD:
2005, 2013 (both Echo Bridge Entertainment)

Escape to Witch Mountain (1995)

Source:
- *Escape to Witch Mountain* (1968) Alexander Key
- Remake of *Escape to Witch Mountain* (1975)

Writers:
Robert Malcolm Young, Peter Rader

Director:
Peter Rader

Stars:
Robert Vaughn, Elisabeth Moss, Erik von Detten, Lynne Moody

Broadcast:
Apr 29, 1995, ABC

Length:
87 min

Freaky Friday (1995)

Source:
- *Freaky Friday* (1972) Mary Rodgers
- Remake of *Freaky Friday* (1976)

Writers:
Stu Krieger

Director:
Melanie Mayron

Stars:
Shelley Long, Gaby Hoffman, Catlin Adams, Sandra Bernhard

Broadcast:
May 6, 1995, ABC

Length:
86 min

The Four Diamonds (1995)

Disney Channel Premiere Film

Source:
'The Four Diamonds' (1972) Chris Millard

Writers:
Todd Robinson

Director:
Peter Werner

Stars:
Thomas Guiry, Christine Lahti, Kevin Dunn, Jayne Brook

Broadcast:
Aug 12, 1995, Disney Channel

Length:
96 min

The Barefoot Executive (1995)

Source:
Remake of *The Barefoot Executive* (1971)

Writers:
Lila Garrett, Bernie Kahn, Stu Billett (story), Tracy Newman, Jonathan Stark, Tim Doyle (screenplay)

Director:
Susan Seidelman

Stars:
Jason London, Eddie Albert, Michael Marich, Jay Mohr

Broadcast:
Nov 11, 1995, ABC

Length:
97 min

The Little Riders (1996)

Disney Channel Premiere Film

Source:
The Little Riders (1963) Margaretha Shermin

Writers:
Gerald Di Pego

Director:
Kevin Connor

Stars:
Noley Thornton, Paul Schofield, Rosemary Harris, Malcolm McDowell

Broadcast:
Mar 24, 1996, Disney Channel

Length:
96 min

DVD:
2014 Echo Bridge Home Entertainment

Nightjohn (1996)

Disney Channel Premiere Film

Source:
Nightjohn (1993) Gary Paulsen

Writers:
Bill Cain

Director:
Charles Burnett

Stars:
Beau Bridges, Carl Lumbly, Allison Jones, Lorraine Toussaint

Broadcast:
Jun 1, 1996, Disney Channel

Length:
96 min

Video:
1998 (Hallmark)

DVD:
2005, 2010 Family Adventure Set, 2013 4 Movies with Soul (all Echo Bridge Entertainment)

Digital:
Amazon

Encino Woman (1996)

Source:
Sequel to *Encino Man* (Hollywood Pictures, 1992)

Writers:
Anne Joseph, Shawn Schepps

Director:
Shawn Schepps

Stars:
Katherine Kousi, Corey Parker, Jay Thomas, John Kassir

Broadcast:
Apr 20, 1996, ABC

Length:
90 min

The Christmas Tree (1996)

Source:
The Christmas Tree (1996) Julie Salamon

Writers:
Janet Brownell, Sally Field

Director:
Sally Field

Stars:
Julie Harris, Andrew McCarthy, Trini Alvarado, Suzi Hofrichter

Broadcast:
Dec 22, 1996, ABC

Length:
93 min

Beverly Hills Family Robinson (1997)

Source:
- *Swiss Family Robinson* (1812) Johann David Wyss
- Remake of *Swiss Family Robinson* (1960)

Writers:
T.C. Smith

Director:
Troy Miller

Stars:
Martin Mull, Dyan Cannon, Sarah Michelle Gellar, Ryan O'Donohue

Broadcast:
Jan 25, 1997, ABC

Length:
88 min

Video:
2001

DVD:
2006 (UK)

Northern Lights (1997)

Disney Channel Original Movie

Source:
Northern Lights stage play (1988) John Hoffman

Writers:
John Hoffman, Kevin Kane

Director:
Linda Yellen

Stars:
Diane Keaton, Joseph Cross, Maury Chaykin, Kathleen York

Broadcast:
Aug 23, 1997, Disney Channel

Length:
95 min

Toothless (1997)

The Wonderful World of Disney

Writers:
Mark S. Kaufman

Director:
Melanie Mayron

Stars:
Kirstie Alley, Dale Midkiff, Ross Malinger, Daryl Mitchell

Broadcast:
Oct 5, 1997, ABC

Length:
92 min

Video:
1998

DVD:
2003

Under Wraps (1997)

Disney Channel Original Movie

Writers:
Don Rhymer

Director:
Greg Beeman

Stars:
Maria Yedidia, Adam Wylie, Clara Bryant, Bill Fagerbakke

Broadcast:
Oct 25, 1997, Disney Channel

Length:
90 min

DVD:
2005 Echo Bridge Entertainment

Digital:
Amazon, iTunes

Tower of Terror (1997)

The Wonderful World of Disney

Source:
The Twilight Zone Tower of Terror theme park attraction

Writers:
D.J. MacHale

Director:
D.J. MacHale

Stars:
Steve Guttenberg, Kirsten Dunst, Nia Peeples, Lindsay Ridgeway

Broadcast:
Oct 26, 1997, ABC

Length:
89 min

Theme Parks:
- Twilight Zone Tower of Terror (HS 1994+), (DCA 2004-2017)
- Tower of Terror (TDS 2006+)
- La Tour de la Terreur: Un Saut dans la Quatrème Dimension (WDS 2007+)

Video:
2001

DVD:
2003, 2012 Disney 4-Movie Collection: Thrills and Chills

Rodgers & Hammerstein's Cinderella (1997)

The Wonderful World of Disney

AKA:
Cinderella

Source:
Remake of *Rodgers & Hammerstein's Cinderella* (1957) Non-Disney TV Movie

Writers:
Robert L. Freedman

Director:
Robert Iscove

Stars:
Brandy, Whitney Houston, Whoopi Goldberg, Victor Garber

Broadcast:
Nov 2, 1997, ABC

Length:
88 min

DVD:
1999, 2003

Angels in the Endzone (1997)

The Wonderful World of Disney

Source:
Sequel to *Angels in the Outfield* (1994)

Writers:
Alan Eisenstock, Larry Mintz

Director:
Gary Nadeau

Stars:
Christopher Lloyd, Matthew Lawrence, David Gallegher, Paul Dooley

Broadcast:
Nov 9, 1997, ABC

Length:
88 min

DVD:
2004, 2012 Disney 4-Movie Collection: Game Changers

Oliver Twist (1997)

The Wonderful World of Disney

Source:

Oliver Twist (1837-1839) Charles Dickens

Writers:

Monte Merrick

Director:

Tony Bill

Stars:

Richard Dreyfuss, Elijah Wood, David O'Hara, Alex Trench

Broadcast:

Nov 16, 1997, ABC

Length:

91 min

Video:

1998

DVD:

2004

The Love Bug (1997)

The Wonderful World of Disney

Source:

Remake/sequel to *The Love Bug* (1969)

Writers:

Ryan Rowe

Director:

Peyton Reed

Stars:

Bruce Campbell, John Hannah, Alexandra Wentworth, Kevin J. O'Connor

Broadcast:

Nov 30, 1997, ABC

Length:

88 min

Video:

2001

Flash (1997)

The Wonderful World of Disney

Writers:
Monte Merrick

Director:
Simon Wincer

Stars:
Lucas Black, Brian Kerwin, Shawn Toovey, Tom Nowicki

Broadcast:
Dec 21, 1997, ABC

Length:
90 min

Video:
2001

Principal Takes a Holiday (1998)

The Wonderful World of Disney

Writers:
Robert King (story/screenplay), Paul Wolff (story)

Director:
Robert King

Stars:
Kevin Nealon, Zachary Ty Bryan, Jessica Steen, Rashaan H. Nall

Broadcast:
Jan 4, 1998, ABC

Length:
96 min

Video:
2000

Ruby Bridges (1998)

The Wonderful World of Disney

Writers:
Toni Ann Johnson

Director:
Euzhan Palcy

Stars:
Chaz Monét, Penelope Ann Miller, Kevin Pollack, Michael Beach

Broadcast:
Jan 18, 1998, ABC

Length:
96 min

Video:
2000

DVD:
2004

Digital:
Amazon, iTunes, Vudu

The Garbage Picking Field Goal Kicking Philadelphia Phenomenon (1998)

The Wonderful World of Disney

Writers:
Tim Kelleher, Greg Fields

Director:
Tim Kelleher

Stars:
Tony Danza, Jessica Tuck, Art LaFleur, Jaime Cardriche

Broadcast:
Feb 15, 1998, ABC

Length:
78 min

Video:
1998

Goldrush: A Real Life Alaskan Adventure (1998)

The Wonderful World of Disney

Writers:
Jacqueline Feather, David Seidler

Director:
John Power

Stars:
Alyssa Milano, W. Morgan Sheppard, Bruce Campbell, Stan Cahill

Broadcast:
Mar 8, 1998, ABC

Length:
96 min
Video:
2001
DVD:
2011 Disney Generations Collection

Mr. Headmistress (1998)

The Wonderful World of Disney

Writers:
Scott Davis Jones, David Kukoff, Matt Roshkow
Director:
James Frawley
Stars:
Harland Williams, Shawna Waldron, Duane Martin, Joel Brooks
Broadcast:
Mar 15, 1998, ABC
Length:
96 min
Video:
2000

Safety Patrol (1998)

The Wonderful World of Disney

Writers:
Savage Steve Holland (story/screenplay), Doug Draizin (story)
Director:
Savage Steve Holland
Stars:
Leslie Nielsen, Bug Hall, Lainie Kazan, Curtis Armstrong
Broadcast:
Mar 29, 1998, ABC
Length:
96 min
Video:
2000

Tourist Trap (1998)
The Wonderful World of Disney

Writers:
Andy Breckman

Director:
Richard Benjamin

Stars:
Daniel Stern, Julie Hagerty, David Rasche, Paul Giamatti

Broadcast:
Apr 5, 1998, ABC

Length:
89 min

Video:
2001

My Date with the President's Daughter (1998)
The Wonderful World of Disney

Writers:
William Robertson, Alex Zamm

Director:
Alex Zamm

Stars:
Dabney Coleman, Will Friedle, Elisabeth Harnois, Mimi Kuzyk

Broadcast:
Apr 19, 1998, ABC

Length:
90 min

Video:
2001

Miracle at Midnight (1998)
The Wonderful World of Disney

Source:
Based on real events

Writers:
Chris Bryant, Monte Merrick

Director:
Ken Cameron

Stars:
Sam Waterston, Mia Farrow, Justin Whalin, Patrick Malahide

Broadcast:
May 17, 1998, ABC

Length:
90 min

Video:
2000

DVD:
2004

Digital:
Amazon, iTunes, Vudu

Soundtrack:
1998 (CD)

You Lucky Dog (1998)

Disney Channel Original Movie

Writers:
David Covell (story/screenplay), Peter I. Baloff, Dave Wollert (screenplay)

Director:
Paul Schneider

Stars:
Kirk Cameron, Chelsea Noble, James Avery, Christine Healey

Broadcast:
Jun 27, 1998, Disney Channel

Length:
89 min

Digital:
Amazon, iTunes

Brink! (1998)

Disney Channel Original Movie

Writers:
Jeff Schechter

Director:
Greg Beeman

Stars:
Erik von Detten, Patrick Levis, Asher Gold, Christina Vidal

Broadcast:
Aug 29, 1998, Disney Channel

Length:
99 min

Digital:
Amazon

Noah (1998)

The Wonderful World of Disney

Source:
Based on the Biblical story of Noah's Ark

Writers:
Juliet Aires, Keith Giglio, Charles F. Bohl

Director:
Ken Kwapis

Stars:
Tony Danza, Wallace Shawn, Jane Sibbett, John Marshall

Broadcast:
Oct 11, 1998, ABC

Length:
90 min

Video:
2000

Halloweentown (1998)

Disney Channel Original Movie

Writers:
Paul Bernbaum (story/screenplay), Jon Cooksey, Ali Marie Matheson (screenplay)

Director:
Duwayne Dunham

Stars:
Debbie Reynolds, Judith Hoag, Robin Thomas, Kimberly J. Brown

Broadcast:
Oct 17, 1998, Disney Channel

Length:
84 min

TV Movie:
- *Halloweentown II: Kalabar's Revenge* (2001) Sequel
- *Halloweentown High* (2004) Sequel
- *Return to Halloweentown* (2006) Sequel

DVD:
2005 Double Feature

Digital:
Amazon, iTunes

A Knight in Camelot (1998)
The Wonderful World of Disney

Source:
A Connecticut Yankee in King Arthur's Court (1889) Mark Twain

Writers:
Joe Wiesenfeld

Director:
Roger Young

Stars:
Whoopi Goldberg, Michael York, Simon Fenton, Paloma Baeza

Broadcast:
Nov 8, 1998, ABC

Length:
90 min

Video:
2001

DVD:
2005 Disney Movie Club Exclusive, 2009

Murder She Purred:
A Mrs. Murphy Mystery (1998)
The Wonderful World of Disney

Source:
Murder, She Meowed (1996) Rita Mae Brown

Writers:
Ann Lewis Hamilton (story/screenplay), Jim Cox (screenplay)

Director:
Simon Wincer

Stars:
Ricki Lake, Blythe Danner, Anthony Clark, Linden Ashby

Broadcast:
Dec 13, 1998, ABC

Length:
88 min

Video:
2001

The New Swiss Family Robinson (1999)

The Wonderful World of Disney

Source:
The Swiss Family Robinson (1812) Johann David Wyss

Writers:
Stewart Raffill

Director:
Stewart Raffill

Stars:
Jane Seymour, David Carradine, James Keach, Jamie Renee Smith

Broadcast:
Jan 10, 1999, ABC

Length:
90 min

Video:
2000 (First Look Home Entertainment)

DVD:
2000 (Eaton Entertainment)

Soundtrack:
1999 (CD, UK)

Selma, Lord, Selma (1999)

The Wonderful World of Disney

Source:
Selma, Lord, Selma (1980) Sheyann Webb, Rachel West, Frank Sikora

Writers:
Cynthia Whitcomb

Director:
Charles Burnett

Stars:
Mackenzie Astin, Jurnee Smollett, Clifton Powell, Ella Joyce

Broadcast:
Jan 17, 1999, ABC

Length:
94 min

Video:
2001

DVD:
2004

Zenon: Girl of the 21st Century (1999)

Disney Channel Original Movie

Source:
Zenon: Girl of the 21st Century (1997) Marilyn Sadler

Writers:
Stu Krieger

Director:
Kenneth Johnson

Stars:
Kirsten Storms, Raven-Symoné, Greg Smith, Holly Fulger

Broadcast:
Jan 23, 1999, Disney Channel

Length:
97 min

TV Movies:
- *Zenon: The Zequel* (2001) Sequel
- *Zenon: Z3* (2004) Sequel

Video:
2002

Digital:
Amazon, iTunes

A Saintly Switch (1999)

The Wonderful World of Disney

Writers:
Sally Hampton, Haris Orkin

Director:
Peter Bogdanovich

Stars:
Vivica A. Fox, David Alan Grier, Al Waxman, Scott Owen

Broadcast:
Jan 24, 1999, ABC

Length:
88 min

DVD:
2004

Balloon Farm (1999)

The Wonderful World of Disney

Source:
Harvey Potter's Balloon Farm (1994) Jerdine Nolen

Writers:
Steven Karczynski

Director:
William Dear

Stars:
Rip Torn, Mara Wilson, Roberts Blossom, Laurie Metcalf

Broadcast:
Mar 28, 1999, ABC

Length:
90 min

Video:
2001

DVD:
2004

Digital:
Amazon, Vudu

Can of Worms (1999)

Disney Channel Original Movie

Source:
Can of Worms (1999) Kathy Mackel

Writers:
Kathy Mackel

Director:
Paul Scheider

Stars:
Michael Shulman, Adam Wylie, Marcus Tanner, Erika Christensen

Broadcast:
Apr 10, 1999, Disney Channel

Length:
88 min

Video:
2001

Digital:
Amazon, iTunes

The Thirteenth Year (1999)

Disney Channel Original Movie

Writers:
Jenny Arata (story/screenplay), Robert L. Baird, Kelly Senecal (screenplay)

Director:
Duwayne Dunham

Stars:
Chez Starbuck, Dave Coulier, Lisa Stahl Sullivan, Brent Briscoe

Broadcast:
May 15, 1999, Disney Channel

Length:
95 min

Video:
2001

Digital:
Amazon, iTunes

Smart House (1999)

Disney Channel Original Movie

Source:
'The Veldt' (1950) Ray Bradbury

Writers:
William Hudson, Stu Krieger

Director:
LeVar Burton

Stars:
Katey Sagal, Ryan Merriman, Kevin Kilner, Jessica Steen
Broadcast:
Jun 26, 1999, Disney Channel
Length:
82 min
Video:
2000
DVD:
2006 Disney Movie Club Exclusive, 2009
Digital:
Amazon, iTunes

Johnny Tsunami (1999)

Disney Channel Original Movie

Writers:
Ann Knapp, Douglas Sloan
Director:
Steve Boyum
Stars:
Brandon Baker, Cary-Hiroyuki Tagawa, Kirsten Storms, Lee Thompson Young
Broadcast:
Jul 24, 1999, Disney Channel
Length:
88 min
TV Movie:
Johnny Kapahala: Back on Board (2007) Sequel
Video:
2002
DVD:
2004 (Australia)
Digital:
Amazon, iTunes

Genius (1999)

Disney Channel Original Movie

Writers:
John Rieck (story/screenplay), Jim Lincoln, Dan Studney (screenplay)

Director:
Rod Daniel

Stars:
Trevor Morgan, Emmy Rossum, Charles Fleischer, Peter Keleghan

Broadcast:
Aug 21, 1999, Disney Channel

Length:
82 min

Digital:
Amazon, iTunes

P.U.N.K.S. (1999)

Disney Channel Original Movie

Writers:
Mark Cramer (story/screenplay), Sean McNamara (story)

Director:
Sean McNamara

Stars:
Randy Quaid, Tim Redwine, Henry Winkler, Kenneth Brown IV

Broadcast:
Sep 4, 1999, Disney Channel

Length:
94 min

Video:
2003 (Allumination)

DVD:
2005 (Allumination), 2011 Triple Feature (Mill Creek Entertainment)

H-E Double Hockey Sticks (1999)

The Wonderful World of Disney

Source:
Griffelkin opera (1955) Lucas Foss, Alastair Reid

Writers:
David Kukoff, Matt Roshkow

Director:
Randall Miller

Stars:
Will Friedle, Matthew Lawrence, Gabrielle Union, Shawn Pyfrom

Broadcast:
Oct 3, 1999, ABC

Length:
96 min

Don't Look Under the Bed (1999)

Disney Channel Original Movie

Writers:
Mark Edward Edens

Director:
Kenneth Johnson

Stars:
Erin Chambers, Ty Hodges, Jake Sakson, Robin Riker

Broadcast:
Oct 9, 1999, Disney Channel

Length:
92 min

Digital:
Amazon, iTunes

Annie (1999)

The Wonderful World of Disney

Source:
Annie musical (1977) Martin Charnin, Thomas Meehan, Charles Strouse

Writers:
Irene Mecchi

Director:
Rob Marshall

Stars:
Kathy Bates, Alicia Morton, Alan Cumming, Audra McDonald

Broadcast:
Nov 7, 1999, ABC

Length:
90 min

Video:
2001

DVD:
2000

Digital:
Amazon, iTunes, Vudu
Soundtrack:
1999 (CD)

Horse Sense (1999)

Disney Channel Original Movie

Writers:
Chad Hayes, Carey W. Hayes
Director:
Greg Beeman
Stars:
Andrew Lawrence, Joey Lawrence, Susan Walters, M.C. Gainey
Broadcast:
Nov 20, 1999, Disney Channel
Length:
92 min
TV Movie:
Jumping Ship (2001) Sequel
Digital:
Amazon, iTunes

PART TEN

2000–2004

The Loretta Claiborne Story (2000)
The Wonderful World of Disney
Source:
Life of Loretta Claiborne (b.1953)
Writers:
Grace McKeaney
Director:
Lee Grant
Stars:
Kimberly Elise, Tina Lifford, Nicole Ari Parker, Damon Gupton
Broadcast:
Jan 16, 2000, ABC
Length:
90 min
Video:
2001
DVD:
2003 Classroom Edition

Up, Up, and Away (2000)
Disney Channel Original Movie
Writers:
Dan Berendsen
Director:
Robert Townsend
Stars:
Robert Townsend, Michael J. Pagan, Alex Datcher, Sherman Hemsley

Broadcast:
Jan 22, 2000, Disney Channel
Length:
90 min
Digital:
Amazon, iTunes

The Color of Friendship (2000)

Disney Channel Original Movie

Source:
Based on a true story
Writers:
Paris Qualles
Director:
Kevin Hooks
Stars:
Carl Lumbly, Penny Johnson, Lindsay Haun, Shadia Simmons
Broadcast:
Feb 5, 2000, Disney Channel
Length:
87 min
Video:
2002
DVD:
2012 Classroom Edition
Digital:
Amazon, iTunes

New True-Life Adventures (2000)

Episodes:
- *Alaska: Dances of the Caribou*
- *Elephant Journey*
- *Sea of Sharks*
- *The Everglades: Home of the Living Dinosaurs*

Broadcast:
Feb 14, 2000+, Syndication
Length:
4 x 45 mins

DVD:
2012 Classroom Edition (individual episodes)

Life-Size (2000)

The Wonderful World of Disney

Writers:
Stephanie Moore (story/screenplay), Mark Rosman (screenplay)

Director:
Mark Rosman

Stars:
Lindsay Lohan, Tyra Banks, Jere Burns, Ann Marie Loder

Broadcast:
Mar 5, 2000, ABC

Length:
101 min

TV Movie:
Life-Size 2 (2018) Sequel

Video:
2000

DVD:
2000, 2009 Double Feature

Model Behavior (2000)

The Wonderful World of Disney

Source:
Janine and Alex, Alex and Janine (1997) Michael Levin

Writers:
David Kukoff, Matt Roshkow

Director:
Mark Rosman

Stars:
Maggie Lawson, Kathie Lee Gifford, Justin Timberlake, Daniel Clark

Broadcast:
Mar 12, 2000, ABC

Length:
85 min

Video:
2000

Alley Cats Strike! (2000)

Disney Channel Original Movie

Writers:

Gregory K. Pincus

Director:

Rod Daniel

Stars:

Kyle Schmid, Robert Ri'chard, Kaley Cuoco, Mimi Paley

Broadcast:

Mar 18, 2000, Disney Channel

Length:

87 min

Video:

2001

Digital:

Amazon, iTunes

Mail to the Chief (2000)

The Wonderful World of Disney

Writers:

Jack Thomas (story), Eric Champnella (story/screenplay)

Director:

Eric Champnella

Stars:

Randy Quaid, Bill Switzer, Holland Taylor, Dave Nichols

Broadcast:

Apr 2, 2000, ABC

Length:

89 min

Video:

2000

DVD:

2005 Disney Movie Club Exclusive

Angels in the Infield (2000)

The Wonderful World of Disney

Source:

Second sequel to *Angels in the Outfield* (1994)

Writers:
Holly Goldberg Sloan (story), Robert King (story/screenplay), Garrett K. Schiff (screenplay)
Director:
Robert King
Stars:
Patrick Warburton, Brittney Irvin, Kurt Fuller, Rebecca Jenkins
Broadcast:
Apr 9, 2000, ABC
Length:
87 min
Video:
2000
DVD:
2004, 2009 Double Feature, 2012 Disney 4-Movie Collection: Game Changers

Rip Girls (2000)

Disney Channel Original Movie
Writers:
Jeanne Rosenberg
Director:
Joyce Chopra
Stars:
Camilla Belle, Dwier Brown, Stacie Hess, Brian Christopher Mark
Broadcast:
Apr 22, 2000, Disney Channel
Length:
87 min
Digital:
Amazon, iTunes

Geppetto (2000)

The Wonderful World of Disney
Source:
The Adventures of Pinocchio (1883) Carlo Collodi
Writers:
David I. Stern

Director:
Tom Moore

Stars:
Drew Carey, Julia Louis-Dreyfus, Brent Spiner, Rene Auberjonois

Broadcast:
May 7, 2000, ABC

Length:
89 min

Video:
2000

DVD:
2005 Disney Movie Club Exclusive, 2009

Soundtrack:
2000 (CD)

Miracle in Lane 2 (2000)

Disney Channel Original Movie

Writers:
Joel Kauffmann, Donald C. Yost

Director:
Greg Beeman

Stars:
Frankie Muniz, Rick Rossovich, Molly Hagan, Patrick Levis

Broadcast:
May 13, 2000, Disney Channel

Length:
89 min

Video:
2002

DVD:
2004

Digital:
Amazon, iTunes

Stepsister from Planet Weird (2000)

Disney Channel Original Movie

Source:
Stepsister from Planet Weird (1996) Francess Lantz

Writers:
Chris Matheson

Director:
Steve Boyum

Stars:
Courtnee Draper, Tamara Hope, Khystyne Haje, Lance Guest

Broadcast:
Jun 17, 2000, Disney Channel

Length:
85 min

Digital:
Amazon, iTunes

Ready to Run (2000)

Disney Channel Original Movie

Writers:
John Wierick

Director:
Duwayne Dunham

Stars:
Krissy Perez, Nestor Serrano, Theresa Saldana, Lillian Hurst

Broadcast:
Jul 14, 2000, Disney Channel

Length:
96 min

Digital:
Amazon, iTunes

The Pooch and the Pauper (2000)

The Wonderful World of Disney

Source:
The Prince and the Pauper (1881) Mark Twain

Writers:
Mark Steilen, Bennett Yellin

Director:
Alex Zamm

Stars:
Richard Karn, Fred Willard, George Wendt, Cody Jones

Broadcast:
Jul 16, 2000, Disney Channel

Length:
88 min

Video:
2000

The New Adventures of Spin and Marty: Suspect Behavior (2000)

The Wonderful World of Disney

Source:
- *The Undertaker's Gone Bananas* (1978) Paul Zindel
- Spin-off of 'The Adventures of Spin and Marty' (1955-1956) Mickey Mouse Club

Writers:
David Simkins

Director:
Rusty Cundieff

Stars:
David Gallagher, Jeremy Foley, Charles Shaughnessy, Judd Nelson

Broadcast:
Aug 13, 2000, ABC

Length:
88 min

Video:
2001

Quints (2000)

Disney Channel Original Movie

Writers:
Matthew Weisman (story/screenplay), Greg Pincus (screenplay)

Director:
Bill Corcoran

Stars:
Kimberly J. Brown, Daniel Roebuck, Elizabeth Morehead, Shadia Simmons

Broadcast:
Aug 18, 2000, Disney Channel

Length:
83 min
Digital:
Amazon, iTunes

The Other Me (2000)

Disney Channel Original Movie
Source:
Me Two (1991) Mary C. Ryan
Writers:
Jeff Schechter
Director:
Manny Coto
Stars:
Andrew Lawrence, Brenden Jefferson, Lori Hallier, Mark Taylor
Broadcast:
Sep 8, 2000, Disney Channel
Length:
90 min
Digital:
Amazon, iTunes

Mom's Got a Date with a Vampire (2000)

Disney Channel Original Movie
Writers:
Lindsay Naythons (story), Robert Keats (screenplay)
Director:
Steve Boyum
Stars:
Caroline Rhea, Charles Shaughnessy, Matthew O'Leary, Laura Vandervoort
Broadcast:
Oct 13, 2000, Disney Channel
Length:
85 min
Digital:
Amazon, iTunes

Phantom of the Megaplex (2000)

Disney Channel Original Movie

Writers:
Stu Krieger

Director:
Blair Treu

Stars:
Taylor Handley, Jacob Smith, Caitlin Wachs, Corinne Bohrer

Broadcast:
Nov 10, 2000, Disney Channel

Length:
89 min

Digital:
Amazon, iTunes

The Miracle Worker (2000)

The Wonderful World of Disney

Source:
The Miracle Worker play (1957) William Gibson

Writers:
Monte Merrick

Director:
Nadia Tass

Stars:
Hallie Kate Eisenberg, Alison Elliott, David Strathairn, Lucas Black

Broadcast:
Nov 12, 2000, ABC

Length:
95 min

Video:
2001

DVD:
2001, 2009 The Shout Factory

Digital:
Amazon, iTunes, Vudu

Santa Who? (2000)

The Wonderful World of Disney

Source:
Unpublished story by Chad Hoffman, Robert Schwartz

Writers:
Debra Frank, Steve L. Hayes

Director:
William Dear

Stars:
Leslie Nielsen, Steven Eckholdt, Robyn Lively, Tommy Davidson

Broadcast:
Nov 19, 2000, ABC

Length:
92 min

Video:
2001

DVD:
2001, 2011 Double Feature/Mill Creek Entertainment

Digital:
Amazon, iTunes, Vudu

The Ultimate Christmas Present (2000)

Disney Channel Original Movie

Writers:
Hallie Einhorn (story), Michael Hitchcock (story/screenplay)

Director:
Greg Beeman

Stars:
Hallee Hirsh, Brenda Song, Peter Scolari, Hallie Todd

Broadcast:
Dec 1, 2000, Disney Channel

Length:
75 min

Digital:
Amazon, iTunes

Zenon: The Zequel (2001)

Disney Channel Original Movie

Source:
Sequel to *Zenon: Girl of the 21st Century* (1999) TV Movie

Writers:
Stu Krieger

Director:
Manny Coto

Stars:
Kirsten Storms, Shadia Simmons, Holly Fulger, Phillip Rhys

Broadcast:
Jan 12, 2001, Disney Channel

Length:
88 min

Video:
2002

Digital:
Amazon, iTunes

Motocrossed (2001)

Disney Channel Original Movie

Writers:
Ann Austen, Douglas Sloan

Director:
Steve Boyum

Stars:
Alana Austin, Mary-Margaret Humes, Trever O'Brien, Timothy Carhart

Broadcast:
Feb 2, 2001, Disney Channel

Length:
91 min

Video:
2002

Digital:
Amazon, iTunes

The Luck of the Irish (2001)

Disney Channel Original Movie

Writers:
Andrew Price (story/screenplay), Mark Edward Edens (screenplay)

Director:
Paul Hoen

Stars:
Ryan Merriman, Alexis Lopez, Glenndon Chatman, Marita Geraghty

Broadcast:
Mar 9, 2001, Disney Channel

Length:
86 min

Video:
2003

Digital:
Amazon, iTunes

Princess of Thieves (2001)

The Wonderful World of Disney

Source:
Legend of Robin Hood

Writers:
Robin Lerner

Director:
Peter Hewitt

Stars:
Malcolm McDowell, Stuart Wilson, Jonathan Hyde, Keira Knightley

Broadcast:
Mar 11, 2001, ABC

Length:
88 min

Video:
2001

DVD:
2005

Bailey's Mistake (2001)

The Wonderful World of Disney

Writers:
Oliver Goldstick

Director:
Michael M. Robin

Stars:
Linda Hamilton, Joan Plowright, Kyle Secor, Jesse James

Broadcast:
Mar 18, 2001, ABC

Length:
90 min

Hounded (2001)

Disney Channel Original Movie

Writers:
Don Calame, Chris Conroy

Director:
Neal Israel

Stars:
Tahj Mowry, Craig Kirkwood, Shia LaBeouf, Ed Begley, Jr.

Broadcast:
Apr 13, 2001, Disney Channel

Length:
91 min

Digital:
Amazon, iTunes

Ladies and the Champ (2001)

The Wonderful World of Disney

Source:
The Last of Jane Austen play (?) Shirl Hendryx

Writers:
Jeff Berry, Shirl Hendryx

Director:
Jeff Barry

Stars:
Olympia Dukakis, Marion Ross, David DeLuise, Sarah Strange

Broadcast:

Apr 22, 2001, ABC

Length:

80 min

Child Star: The Shirley Temple Story (2001)

The Wonderful World of Disney

Source:

Child Star: An Autobiography (1988) Shirley Temple Black

Writers:

Joe Wiesenfeld

Director:

Nadia Tass

Stars:

Ashley Rose Orr, Emily Anne Hart, Connie Britton, Colin Friels

Broadcast:

May 13, 2001, ABC

Length:

88 min

DVD:

2001

Jett Jackson: The Movie (2001)

Disney Channel Original Movie

Source:

Sequel to *The Famous Jett Jackson* (1998-2001) Disney Channel TV Series

Writers:

Bruce Kalish

Director:

Shawn Levy

Stars:

Lee Thompson Young, Lindy Booth, Nigel Shawn Williams, Ryan Sommers Baum

Broadcast:

Jun 8, 2001, Disney Channel

Length:

89 min

Video:
2002
Digital:
Amazon, iTunes

The Jennie Project (2001)

Disney Channel Original Movie

Source:
Jennie (1994) Douglas Preston

Writers:
Charles Leavitt, Gary Nadeau

Director:
Gary Nadeau

Stars:
Alex D. Linz, Lance Guest, Sheila Kelley, Sheryl Lee Ralph

Broadcast:
Jul 13, 2001, Disney Channel

Length:
76 min

Digital:
Amazon, iTunes

Soundtrack:
2001 (CD)

Jumping Ship (2001)

Disney Channel Original Movie

Source:
Sequel to *Horse Sense* (1999) TV Movie

Writers:
Chad Hayes, Carey W. Hayes

Director:
Michael Lange

Stars:
Andrew Lawrence, Joey Lawrence, Matt Lawrence, Susan Walters

Broadcast:
Aug 17, 2001, Disney Channel

Length:
92 min

DVD:
2006 Disney Movie Club Exclusive
Digital:
Amazon, iTunes

The Poof Point (2001)
Disney Channel Original Movie
Source:
The Poof Point (1992) Ellen Weiss
Writers:
Stu Krieger
Director:
Neal Israel
Stars:
Tahj Mowry, Dawnn Lewis, Raquel Lee, Mary Curry
Broadcast:
Sep 14, 2001, Disney Channel
Length:
79 min
Digital:
Amazon, iTunes

Walt: The Man Behind the Myth (2001)
The Wonderful World of Disney
Writers:
Katherine Greene, Richard Greene, Jean-Pierre Isbouts
Director:
Jean-Pierre Isbouts
Broadcast:
Sep 16, 2001, ABC
Length:
87 min
Video:
2002
DVD:
2004, 2012

Halloweentown II: Kalabar's Revenge (2001)

Disney Channel Original Movie

Source:
Sequel to *Halloweentown* (1998) TV Movie

Writers:
Jon Cooksey, Ali Marie Matheson

Director:
Mary Lambert

Stars:
Debbie Reynolds, Kimberly J. Brown, Judith Hoag, Daniel Kountz

Broadcast:
Oct 12, 2001, Disney Channel

Length:
81 min

DVD:
2005 Double Feature

Digital:
Amazon, iTunes

The Facts of Life Reunion (2001)

The Wonderful World of Disney

Source:
Sequel to *The Facts of Life* (1979-1988) Non-Disney TV series

Writers:
Max Enscoe, Annie DeYoung (story/screenplay), Deborah Dean Davis (screenplay)

Director:
Charles Herman-Wurmfeld

Stars:
Lisa Whelchel, Kim Fields, Mindy Cohn, Charlotte Rae

Broadcast:
Nov 18, 2001, ABC

Length:
90 min

Brian's Song (2001)

The Wonderful World of Disney

Source:
I am Third (1970) Gale Sayers, Al Silverman

Remake of *Brian's Song* (1971) Non-Disney movie

Writers:
William Blinn (story), John Gray, Allen Clare (screenplay)

Director:
John Gray

Stars:
Sean Maher, Mekhi Phifer, Ben Gazzara, Paula Cale

Broadcast:
Dec 2, 2001, ABC

Length:
88 min

Video/DVD:
2002 Columbia TriStar

Digital:
Amazon, iTunes

'Twas the Night (2001)

Disney Channel Original Movie

Writers:
Jim Lincoln, Dan Studney (story/screenplay), Jenny Tripp (screenplay)

Director:
Nick Castle

Stars:
Bryan Cranston, Josh Zuckerman, Jefferson Mappin, Brenda Grate

Broadcast:
Dec 7, 2001, Disney Channel

Length:
84 min

Digital:
Amazon, iTunes

Double Teamed (2002)

Disney Channel Original Movie

Source:
True story of Heather and Mary Burge (b.1971)

Writers:
Douglas Penn (story), John Wierick (story/screenplay)

Director:
Duwayne Dunham

Stars:
Poppi Monroe, Annie McElwain, Mackenzie Phillips, Nicky Searcy

Broadcast:
Jan 18, 2002, Disney Channel

Length:
93 min

Video:
2002

Digital:
Amazon, iTunes

Cadet Kelly (2002)

Disney Channel Original Movie

Writers:
Gail Parent, Michael Walsh

Director:
Larry Shaw

Stars:
Hilary Duff, Gary Cole, Christy Carlson Romano, Shawn Ashmore

Broadcast:
Mar 8, 2002, Disney Channel

Length:
101 min

Video/DVD:
2005

Digital:
Amazon, iTunes, Netflix

Tru Confessions (2002)

Disney Channel Original Movie

Source:
Tru Confessions (1997) Janet Tashjian

Writers:
Stu Krieger

Director:
Paul Hoen

Stars:
Clara Bryant, Shia LaBeouf, Mare Winningham, William Francis McGuire

Broadcast:
Apr 5, 2002, Disney Channel

Length:
83 min

Digital:
Amazon, iTunes

Get a Clue (2002)

Disney Channel Original Movie

Writers:
Alana Sanko

Director:
Maggie Greenwald

Stars:
Lindsay Lohan, Bug Hall, Brenda Song, Ali Mukaddam

Broadcast:
Jun 28, 2002, Disney Channel

Length:
83 min

DVD:
2005, 2009 Double Feature

Digital:
Amazon, iTunes

Gotta Kick It Up! (2002)

Disney Channel Original Movie

Writers:
Megan Cole (story), Nancy De Los Santos (story/screenplay), Ramón Menéndez, Tom Musca, Stu Krieger (screenplay)

Director:
Ramón Menéndez

Stars:
Susan Egan, Camile Guaty, America Ferrera, Sabrina Wiener

Broadcast:
Jul 26, 2002, Disney Channel

Length:
78 min

Digital:
Amazon, iTunes

A Ring of Endless Light (2002)

Disney Channel Original Movie

Source:
A Ring of Endless Light (1980) Madeleine L'Engle

Writers:
Marita Giovanni, Bruce Graham

Director:
Greg Beeman

Stars:
Mischa Barton, Ryan Merriman, Jared Padelecki, James Whitmore

Broadcast:
Aug 23, 2002, Disney Channel

Length:
88 min

Digital:
Amazon, iTunes

The Scream Team (2002)

Disney Channel Original Movie

Writers:
Robert Short (story), Dan Berendsen (story/screenplay)

Director:
Stuart Gillard

Stars:
Tommy Davidson, Kathy Najimy, Eric Idle, Mark Rendall

Broadcast:
Oct 4, 2002, Disney Channel

Length:
87 min

Digital:
Amazon, iTunes

You Wish! (2003)

Disney Channel Original Movie

Source:
If I Had One Wish (1991) Jackie French Koller

Writers:
Christopher Reed, Cynthia Carle

Director:
Paul Hoen

Stars:
A.J. Trauth, Spencer Breslin, Lalaine, Tim Reid

Broadcast:
Jan 10, 2003, Disney Channel

Length:
84 min

Digital:
Amazon

Sounder (2003)
The Wonderful World of Disney

Source:
Sounder (1969) William H. Armstrong

Writers:
Bill Cain

Director:
Kevin Hooks

Stars:
Carl Lumbly, Suzanne Douglas, Daniel Lee Robertson III, Paul Winfield

Broadcast:
Jan 19, 2003, Disney Channel

Length:
96 min

Video/DVD:
2003

The Music Man (2003)
The Wonderful World of Disney

AKA:
Meredith Willson's The Music Man

Source:
The Music Man stage musical (1957) Meredith Willson, Franklin Lacey

Writers:
Sally Robinson

Director:
Jeff Bleckner

Stars:
Matthew Broderick, Kristin Chenoweth, Victor Garber, Debra Monk

Broadcast:
Feb 16, 2003, ABC

Length:
132 min

Video/DVD:
2003

Digital:
Amazon, iTunes, Vudu

Soundtrack:
2003 (CD)

Right on Track (2003)

Disney Channel Original Movie

Source:
True story of Erica (b.1983) and Courtney (b.1986) Enders

Writers:
Sally Nemeth, Bruce Graham

Director:
Duwayne Dunham

Stars:
Beverley Mitchell, Jon Robert Lindstrom, Brie Larson, Marcus Toji

Broadcast:
Mar 21, 2003, Disney Channel

Length:
89 min

Digital:
Amazon, iTunes

A Wrinkle in Time (2003)

The Wonderful World of Disney

Source:
A Wrinkle in Time (1962) Madeleine L'Engle

Writers:
Susan Shilliday

Director:
John Kent Harrison

Stars:
Alfre Woodard, Kate Nelligan, Alison Elliott, Kyle Secor

Broadcast:
Apr 25, 2003 (Canada)
May 10, 2004, ABC (USA)

Length:
128 min

Movies:
A Wrinkle in Time (2018) Based on same book

DVD:
2004 Disney, 2011 Echo Bridge Entertainment + Double Feature, 2017 Lionsgate Films

Digital:
Amazon, iTunes, Vudu

Eloise at the Plaza (2003)

The Wonderful World of Disney

Source:
Eloise book series (1955-2002) Kay Thompson

Writers:
Janet Brownell

Director:
Kevin Lima

Stars:
Julie Andrews, Sofia Vassilieva, Jeffrey Tambor, Christine Baranski

Broadcast:
Apr 27, 2003, ABC

Length:
89 min

TV Movie:
Eloise at Christmastime (2003) Sequel

Video/DVD:
2003

Soundtrack:
2006 Intrada (CD)

The Even Stevens Movie (2003)

Disney Channel Original Movie

Source:
Follows *Even Stevens* (2000-2003) Disney Channel TV series

Writers:
Dennis Rinsler, Marc Warren

Director:
Sean McNamara

Stars:
Shia LaBeouf, Christy Carlson Romano, Nick Spano, Tom Virtue

Broadcast:
Jun 13, 2003, Disney Channel

Length:
93 min

Video/DVD:
2005

Digital:
Amazon, iTunes

Eddie's Million Dollar Cook-Off (2003)

Disney Channel Original Movie

Writers:
Jack Jason, Rick Bitzelberger (story), Dan Berendsen (story/screenplay)

Director:
Paul Hoen

Stars:
Taylor Ball, Orlando Brown, Reiley McClendon, Rose McIver

Broadcast:
Jul 18, 2003, Disney Channel

Length:
85 min

Digital:
Amazon, iTunes

The Cheetah Girls (2003)

Disney Channel Original Movie

Source:
The Cheetah Girls series (1999-2002) Deborah Gregory

Writers:
Alison Taylor

Director:
Oz Scott

Stars:
Raven-Symoné, Lynn Whitfield, Adrienne Bailon, Kiely Williams

Broadcast:
Aug 15, 2003, Disney Channel

Length:
93 min

TV Movies:
- *The Cheetah Girls 2* (2006) Sequel
- *The Cheetah Girls: One World* (2008) Sequel

Video Games:
- *The Cheetah Girls* (2006) GBA
- *The Cheetah Girls: Pop Star Sensations* (2007) DS
- *The Cheetah Girls: Passport to Stardom* (2008) DS

Video/DVD:
2004

Digital:
Amazon, iTunes, Netflix

Soundtrack:
2003, 2004 Special Edition (CD)

Phenomenon II (2003)

The Wonderful World of Disney

Source:
Sequel to *Phenomenon* (1996) Touchstone Pictures movie

Writers:
Gerald Di Pego

Director:
Ken Olin

Stars:
Christopher Shyer, Jill Clayburgh, Peter Coyote, Terry O'Quinn

Broadcast:
Nov 1, 2003, ABC

Length:
82 min

Full-Court Miracle (2003)

Disney Channel Original Movie

Source:
True story of Lamont Carr (1952-2017)

Writers:
Joel Silverman, Joel Kauffmann, Donald C. Yost

Director:
Stuart Gillard

Stars:
Alex D. Linz, Richard T. Jones, R.H. Thomson, Linda Kash

Broadcast:
Nov 21, 2003, Disney Channel

Length:
94 min

Digital:
Amazon, iTunes

Eloise at Christmastime (2003)

The Wonderful World of Disney

Source:
Sequel to *Eloise at the Plaza* (2003) TV movie

Writers:
Elizabeth Chandler

Director:
Kevin Lima

Stars:
Julie Andrews, Sofia Vassilieva, Jeffrey Tambor, Christine Baranski

Broadcast:
Nov 22, 2003, ABC

Length:
89 min

Video/DVD:
2004

Soundtrack:
2006 Intrada (CD)

Kim Possible: A Sitch in Time (2003)

Source:
Spin-off of *Kim Possible* (2002-2007) TV series

Writers:
Bill Motz, Bob Roth

Director:
Steve Loter

Broadcast:
Nov 28, 2003, Disney Channel

Length:
65 min

TV Movie:
- *Kim Possible: So the Drama* (2005) Further spin-off
- *Kim Possible* (2019) Live-action spin-off

DVD:
2004

Pixel Perfect (2004)

Disney Channel Original Movie

Writers:
Alan Sacks (story), Neal Shusterman (story/screenplay)

Director:
Mark A. Z. Dippé

Stars:
Ricky Ullman, Leah Pipes, Spencer Redford, Chris Williams

Broadcast:
Jan 16, 2004, Disney Channel

Length:
85 min

Digital:
Amazon, iTunes

Soundtrack:
2004 (CD)

Going to the Mat (2004)

Disney Channel Original Movie

Writers:
Chris Nolan, Laurie Nolan (story/screenplay), Steve Bloom, Stu Krieger (screenplay)

Director:
Stuart Gillard

Stars:
Andrew Lawrence, Khleo Thomas, Billy Aaron Brown, Brenda Strong

Broadcast:
Mar 19, 2004, Disney Channel

Length:
92 min

Digital:
Amazon, iTunes

Zenon: Z3 (2004)

Disney Channel Original Movie

Source:
Second sequel to *Zenon: Girl of the 21st Century* (1999) TV movie

Writers:
Stu Krieger

Director:
Steve Rash

Stars:
Kirsten Storms, Alyson Morgan, Glenn McMillan, Benjamin J. Easter

Broadcast:
Jun 11, 2004, Disney Channel

Length:
81 min

Digital:
Amazon, iTunes

Soundtrack:
2004 (CD)

Stuck in the Suburbs (2004)

Disney Channel Original Movie

Writers:
Wendy Engelberg, Amy Engelberg (story/screenplay), Dan Berendsen (screenplay)

Director:
Savage Steve Holland

Stars:
Danielle Panabaker, Brenda Song, Taran Killam, Ryan Belleville

Broadcast:
Jul 16, 2004, Disney Channel

Length:
78 min
Digital:
Amazon, iTunes
Soundtrack:
2004 (CD)

Tiger Cruise (2004)

Disney Channel Original Movie
Writers:
Anna Sandor, Bruce Graham
Director:
Duwayne Dunham
Stars:
Bill Pullman, Hayden Panettiere, Bianca Collins, Nathaniel Lee, Jr.
Broadcast:
Aug 6, 2004, Disney Channel
Length:
87 min
Digital:
Amazon, iTunes

Halloweentown High (2004)

Disney Channel Original Movie
Source:
Second sequel to *Halloweentown* (1998) TV movie
Writers:
Dan Berendsen
Director:
Mark A.Z. Dippé
Stars:
Debbie Reynolds, Kimberley J. Brown, Judith Hoag, Joey Zimmerman
Broadcast:
Oct 8, 2004, Disney Channel
Length:
82 min
Video/DVD:
2005
Digital:
Amazon, iTunes

PART ELEVEN

2005–2009

Now You See It... (2005)
Disney Channel Original Movie
Writers:
Bill Fritz
Director:
Duwayne Dunham
Stars:
Alyson Michalka, Johnny Pacar, Frank Langella, Chris Olivero
Broadcast:
Jan 14, 2005, Disney Channel
Length:
83 min
Digital:
Amazon, iTunes

Buffalo Dreams (2005)
Disney Channel Original Movie
Writers:
Marjorie Schwartz Nielsen
Director:
David Jackson
Stars:
Reiley McClendon, Simon R. Baker, Graham Greene, George Newbern
Broadcast:
Mar 11, 2005, Disney Channel
Length:
89 min

Digital:
Amazon, iTunes

Kim Possible: So the Drama (2005)

Disney Channel Original Movie

AKA:
Kim Possible Movie: So the Drama

Source:
Spin-off of *Kim Possible* (2002-2007) TV series

Writers:
Bob Schooley, Mark McCorkle

Director:
Steve Loter

Broadcast:
Apr 8, 2005, Disney Channel

Length:
66 min (Original), 71 min (Extended)

DVD:
2005 Extended Edition

Digital:
Amazon, iTunes

The Muppets' Wizard of Oz (2005)

Source:
The Wizard of Oz (1900) L. Frank Baum

Writers:
Debra Frank, Steve L. Hayes (story/screenplay), Tom Martin, Adam F. Goldberg (screenplay)

Director:
Kirk R. Thatcher

Stars:
Ashanti, Queen Latifah, David Alan Grier, Jeffrey Tambor

Broadcast:
May 20, 2005, ABC

Length:
88 min (Original), 100 min (Extended)

Video/DVD:
2005 (Extended)

Digital:
Amazon, iTunes, Vudu

Soundtrack:
2005 *Best of The Muppets* (CD)

Go Figure (2005)

Disney Channel Original Movie

Writers:
Patrick J. Clifton, Beth Rigazio

Director:
Francine McDougall

Stars:
Jordan Hinson, Whitney Sloan, Amy Halloran, Tania Gunadi

Broadcast:
Jun 10, 2005, Disney Channel

Length:
88 min

Digital:
Amazon, iTunes

Soundtrack:
2005 (CD)

Life is Ruff (2005)

Disney Channel Original Movie

Writers:
Eddie Guzelian

Director:
Charles Haid

Stars:
Kyle Massey, Kay Panabaker, Mitchel Musso, Carter Jenkins

Broadcast:
Jul 15, 2005, Disney Channel

Length:
84 min

Digital:
Amazon, iTunes

The Proud Family Movie (2005)

Disney Channel Original Movie

Source:
Series finale of *The Proud Family* (2001-2005) TV series

Writers:
Ralph Farquhar, Calvin Brown Jr., John Patrick White, Stiles White

Director:
Bruce W. Smith

Broadcast:
Aug 19, 2005, Disney Channel

Length:
94 min

DVD:
2005

Digital:
Amazon, iTunes

Twitches (2005)

Disney Channel Original Movie

Source:
Twitches book series (2001-2004) H.B. Gilmour, Randi Reisfeld

Writers:
Melissa Gould, Dan Berendsen

Director:
Stuart Gillard

Stars:
Tia Mowry, Tamara Mowry, Kristen Wilson, Patrick Fabian

Broadcast:
Oct 14, 2005, Disney Channel

Length:
86 min

TV Movie:
Twitches Too (2007) Sequel

DVD:
2006 Betwitched Edition

Digital:
Amazon, iTunes

Once Upon a Mattress (2005)

The Wonderful World of Disney

Source:
Once Upon a Mattress stage musical (1958), Mary Rodgers, Marshall Barer, Dean Fuller, Jay Thompson

Writers:
Janet Brownell

Director:
Kathleen Marshall

Stars:
Carol Burnett, Tracey Ullman, Denis O'Hare, Zooey Deschanel

Broadcast:
Dec 18, 2005, ABC

Length:
90 min

DVD:
2005

Digital:
Amazon, iTunes, Vudu

High School Musical (2006)

Disney Channel Original Movie

Writers:
Peter Barsocchini

Director:
Kenny Ortega

Stars:
Zac Efron, Vanessa Hudgens, Ashley Tisdale, Lucas Grabeel

Broadcast:
Jan 20, 2006, Disney Channel

Length:
98 min

Comic Books:
- *High School Musical* (2007)
- *High School Musical: Lasting Impressions* (2008)

Movies:
- *High School Musical 3: Senior Year* (2008) Sequel
- *High School Musical: El Desafío* (2008) Argentinian spin-off

- *High School Musical: El Desafío* (2008) Mexican spin-off
- *High School Musical: O Desafio* (2010) Brazilian spin-off
- *High School Musical China* (2010) Chinese spin-off
- *Sharpay's Fabulous Adventure* (DTV, 2011) Spin-off

Stage Musical:
- *High School Musical: The Concert* (2006-2007) [Collection: *High School Musical: The Concert* (2007) DVD/CD]
- *High School Musical on Stage!* (2007+)
- *High School Musical Jr.* (?) Disney Theatrical Licensing

TV Series:
- *High School Musical: Get in the Picture* (2008) Reality TV show
- *High School Musical: The Series* (2019)

TV Movies:
- *High School Musical 2* (2007) Sequel
- *High School Musical 4* (TBC) Sequel

Video Games:
- *High School Musical: Sing It!* (2007) PS2, Wii
- *High School Musical: Makin' the Cut!* (2007) PS2, Wii, DS

DVD*/Blu-ray:
2006 Encore Edition* + Remix Edition*, 2009 Remix, 2011 Remix

Digital:
Amazon, iTunes, Netflix, Vudu

Soundtrack:
2006 + Special Edition, 2007 *Hits Remixed* (CD)

Cow Belles (2006)

Disney Channel Original Movie

Writers:
Matt Dearborn (story/screenplay), Stu Krieger (screenplay)

Director:
Francine McDougall

Stars:
Alyson Michalka, Amanda Michalka, Michael Trevino, Christian Serratos

Broadcast:
Mar 24, 2006, Disney Channel

Length:
90 min
DVD:
2006
Digital:
Amazon, iTunes, Netflix

Wendy Wu: Homecoming Warrior (2006)
Disney Channel Original Movie
Writers:
Vince Cheung, Ben Montanio, B. Mark Seabrooks, Lydia Look
Director:
John Laing
Stars:
Brenda Song, Shin Koyamada, Tsai Chin, Susan Chuang
Broadcast:
Jun 16, 2006, Disney Channel
Length:
91 min
DVD:
2006 Kickin' Edition
Digital:
Amazon, iTunes, Netflix

Leroy & Stitch (2006)
Source:
Sequel to *Lilo & Stitch* (2002) and *Lilo & Stitch: The Series* (2003-2006)
Writers:
Roberts Gannaway, Jess Winfield
Directors:
Roberts Gannaway, Tony Craig
Broadcast:
Jun 23, 2006, Disney Channel
Length:
73 min
DVD:
2006
Digital:
Amazon, iTunes, Vudu

Read It and Weep (2006)

Disney Channel Original Movie

Source:

How My Private, Personal Journal Became a Bestseller (2004) Julia DeVillers

Writers:

Patrick J. Clifton, Beth Rigazio

Director:

Paul Hoen

Stars:

Kay Panabaker, Danielle Panabaker, Alexandra Krosney, Marquise C. Brown

Broadcast:

Jul 21, 2006, Disney Channel

Length:

84 min

DVD:

2007 Zapped Edition

Digital:

Amazon, iTunes, Netflix

The Cheetah Girls 2 (2006)

Disney Channel Original Movie

Source:

Sequel to *The Cheetah Girls* (2003) TV movie

Writers:

Bethesda Brown, Alison Taylor

Director:

Kenny Ortega

Stars:

Raven-Symoné, Adrienne Bailon, Sabrina Bryan, Kiely Williams

Broadcast:

Aug 25, 2006, Disney Channel

Length:

96 min

DVD:

2006 Cheetah-licious Edition

Digital:

Amazon, iTunes, Netflix

Soundtrack:
2006 + Special Edition (CD)

Return to Halloweentown (2006)
Disney Channel Original Movie
Source:
Third sequel to *Halloweentown* (1998) TV movie
Writers:
Max Enscoe, Annie DeYoung, Juliet Giglio, Keith Giglio
Director:
David Jackson
Stars:
Sara Paxton, Summer Bishil, Lucas Grabeel, Judith Hoag
Broadcast:
Oct 20, 2006, Disney Channel
Length:
88 min
DVD:
2007 Ultimate Secret Edition
Digital:
Amazon, iTunes

Jump In! (2007)
Disney Channel Original Movie
Writers:
Doreen Spicer, Regina Hicks, Karin Gist
Director:
Paul Hoen
Stars:
Corbin Bleu, Keke Palmer, David Reivers, Kylee Russell
Broadcast:
Jan 12, 2007, Disney Channel
Length:
85 min
DVD:
2007 Freestyle Edition
Digital:
Amazon, iTunes, Netflix

Soundtrack:
2007 (CD)

Johnny Kapahala: Back on Board (2007)

Disney Channel Original Movie

Source:
Sequel to *Johnny Tsunami* (1999) TV movie

Writers:
Ann Austen, Douglas Sloan, Max Enscoe, Annie DeYoung

Director:
Eric Bross

Stars:
Brandon Baker, Cary Hiroyuki, Jake T. Austin, Rose McIver

Broadcast:
Jun 8, 2007, Disney Channel

Length:
90 min

DVD:
2007

Digital:
Amazon, iTunes

High School Musical 2 (2007)

Disney Channel Original Movie

Source:
Sequel to *High School Musical* (2006) TV movie

Writers:
Peter Barsocchini

Director:
Kenny Ortega

Stars:
Zac Efron, Vanessa Hudgens, Ashley Tisdale, Lucas Grabeel

Broadcast:
Aug 17, 2007, Disney Channel

Length:
104 min (Original), 111 min (Extended)

Stage Musical:
High School Musical 2: On Stage! (2008+)

Video Game:
High School Musical 2: Work This Out! (2008) DS

DVD*/Blu-ray:
2007 Extended Edition, 2008 Deluxe Dance Edition*, 2011 Extended Edition

Digital:
Amazon, iTunes, Netflix

Soundtrack:
2007 + Collector's Edition + *Non-Stop Dance Party* (CD)

Twitches Too (2007)

Disney Channel Original Movie

Source:
Sequel to *Twitches* (2005) TV movie

Writers:
H.B. Gilmour, Randi Reisfeld

Director:
Stuart Gillard

Stars:
Tia Mowry, Tamera Mowry, Kristen Wilson, Jackie Rosenbaum

Broadcast:
Oct 12, 2007, Disney Channel

Length:
83 min

DVD:
2008 Double Charmed Edition

Digital:
Amazon, iTunes

Minutemen (2008)

Disney Channel Original Movie

Writers:
David Diamond, David Weissman (story), John Killoran (screenplay)

Director:
Lev L. Spiro

Stars:
Jason Dolley, Luke Benward, Nicholas Braun, Chelsea Staub

Broadcast:
Jan 25, 2008, Disney Channel

Length:
98 min
DVD:
2008
Digital:
Amazon, iTunes

Camp Rock (2008)

Disney Channel Original Movie
Writers:
Karin Gist, Regina Y. Hicks, Julie Brown, Paul Brown
Director:
Matthew Diamond
Stars:
Demi Lovato, Joe Jonas, Meahgan Martin, Maria Canals-Barrera
Broadcast:
Jun 20, 2008, Disney Channel
Length:
94 min (Original), 98 min (Extended)
Stage Musical:
Camp Rock (2010+)
TV Movie:
Camp Rock 2: The Final Jam (2010) Sequel
TV Series:
My Camp Rock (2009-2010) Reality TV, UK/Scandinavia/Benelux/Spain/France
DVD/Blu-ray:
2008 Extended Rock Star Edition
Digital:
iTunes, Netflix
Soundtrack:
2008 (CD)

The Cheetah Girls: One World (2008)

Disney Channel Original Movie
Source:
Second sequel to *The Cheetah Girls* (2003) TV movie
Writers:
Dan Berendsen (story/screenplay), Jen Small (screenplay)

Director:
Paul Hoen

Stars:
Sabrina Bryan, Adrienne Bailon, Kiely Williams, Roshan Seth

Broadcast:
Aug 22, 2008, Disney Channel

Length:
88 min

DVD/Blu-ray:
2008 Extended Music Edition

Digital:
Amazon, iTunes Netflix

Soundtrack:
2008 (CD)

A Muppets Christmas: Letters to Santa (2008)

Writers:
Paul Williams, Hugh Fink, Scott Ganz, Andrew Samson

Director:
Kirk R. Thatcher

Stars:
Madison Pettis, Whoopi Goldberg, Richard Griffiths, Jane Krakowski

Broadcast:
Dec 17, 2008, NBC

Length:
43 min (Original), 56 min (Extended)

DVD:
2009 Extended Edition

Digital:
Amazon, iTunes, Vudu

Soundtrack:
2009 (Digital EP)

Dadnapped (2009)

Disney Channel Original Movie

Writers:
Alan Silberberg

Director:
Paul Hoen

Stars:
Emily Osment, Jason Earles, Moises Arias, David Henrie

Broadcast:
Feb 16, 2009, Disney Channel

Length:
83 min

DVD:
2009 Double Feature

Digital:
Amazon, iTunes

Hatching Pete (2009)

Disney Channel Original Movie

Writers:
Paul W. Cooper

Director:
Stuart Gillard

Stars:
Jason Dolley, Mitchel Musso, Tiffany Thornton, Josie Loren

Broadcast:
Apr 24, 2009, Disney Channel

Length:
89 min

DVD:
2009 Double Feature

Digital:
Amazon, iTunes

Princess Protection Program (2009)

Disney Channel Original Movie

Writers:
David Morgasen (story), Annie DeYoung (story/screenplay)

Director:
Allison Liddi-Brown

Stars:
Demi Lovato, Selena Gomez, Nicholas Braun, Jamie Chung

Broadcast:
Jun 26, 2009, Disney Channel

Length:
89 min
DVD:
2009 Royal B.F.F. Extended Edition
Digital:
Amazon, iTunes, Netflix

Wizards of Waverly Place: The Movie (2009)
Disney Channel Original Movie
Source:
Spin-off from *Wizards of Waverly Place* (2007-2012) Disney Channel TV
series
Writers:
Dan Berendsen
Director:
Lev L. Spiro
Stars:
Selena Gomez, David Henrie, Jake T. Austin, Jennifer Stone
Broadcast:
Aug 28, 2009, Disney Channel
Length:
94 min (Original), 98 min (Extended)
TV Special:
The Wizards Return: Alex vs. Alex (2013) Disney Channel
DVD:
2009 Extended Edition
Digital:
Amazon, iTunes, Netflix
Soundtrack:
2009 *Wizards of Waverley Place* (CD)

PART TWELVE

2010-2018

StarStruck (2010)

Disney Channel Original Movie

Writers:
Barbara Johns (story/screenplay), Annie DeYoung (screenplay)

Director:
Michael Grossman

Stars:
Sterling Knight, Danielle Campbell, Brandon Mychal Smith, Maggie Castle

Broadcast:
Feb 14, 2010, Disney Channel

Length:
84 min

DVD:
2010 Extended Edition

Digital:
Amazon, iTunes, Netflix

Soundtrack:
2010 (CD)

Harriet the Spy: Blog Wars (2010)

Source:
Harriet the Spy (1964) Louise Fitzhugh

Writers:
Alexandra Clarke, Heather Conkie

Director:
Ron Oliver

Stars:
Jennifer Stone, Kristin Booth, Wesley Morgan, Doug Murray

Broadcast:
Mar 26, 2010, Disney Channel

Length:
87 min

DVD:
2010 (Vivendi Entertainment)

Digital:
Amazon, Netflix

16 Wishes (2010)

Writers:
Annie DeYoung

Director:
Peter DeLuise

Stars:
Debby Ryan, Jean-Luc Bilodeau, Anna Mae Wills, Karissa Tynes

Broadcast:
Jun 25, 2010, Disney Channel

Length:
90 min

DVD*/Blu-ray:
2010 (Image Entertainment), 2014* Debby Ryan Double Feature
(Image Entertainment)

Digital:
Amazon, iTunes, Vudu

Soundtrack:
2010 (CD)

Den Brother (2010)

Disney Channel Original Movie

Writers:
Michael Horowitz (story), Jim Krieg (screenplay)

Director:
Mark L. Taylor

Stars:
Hutch Dano, G. Hannelius, Vicky Lewis, Debra Mooney

Broadcast:
Aug 13, 2010, Disney Channel

Length:
89 min
Digital:
Amazon, iTunes

Camp Rock 2: The Final Jam (2010)

Disney Channel Original Movie
Source:
Sequel to *Camp Rock* (2008) TV movie
Writers:
Dan Berendsen, Karin Gist, Regina Y. Hicks
Director:
Paul Hoen
Stars:
Demi Lovato, Kevin Jones, Joe Jonas, Nick Jonas
Broadcast:
Sep 3, 2010, Disney Channel
Length:
97 min (Original), 104 min (Extended)
Stage Musical:
Camp Rock (2010+) Includes songs from both movies
DVD/Blu-ray:
2010 Extended Edition
Digital:
iTunes, Netflix
Soundtrack:
2010 (CD)

Avalon High (2010)

Disney Channel Original Movie
Source:
Avalon High (2005) Meg Cabot
Writers:
Julie Sherman Wolfe, Amy Talkington
Director:
Stuart Gillard
Stars:
Brittany Robertson, Molly C. Quinn, Gregg Sulkin, Steve Valentine

Broadcast:
Nov 12, 2010, Disney Channel

Length:
89 min

Digital:
Amazon, iTunes

The Suite Life Movie (2011)

Disney Channel Original Movie

Source:
Sequel to *The Suite Life of Zack and Cody* (2005-2008) and *The Suite Life on Deck* (2008-2011) Disney Channel TV series

Writers:
Michael Saltzman, Robert Horn

Director:
Sean McNamara

Stars:
Cole Sprouse, Dylan Sprouse, Debby Ryan, Brenda Song

Broadcast:
Mar 25, 2011, Disney Channel

Length:
79 min

Digital:
Amazon, iTunes

Lemonade Mouth (2011)

Disney Channel Original Movie

Source:
Lemonade Mouth (2007) Mark Peter Hughes

Writers:
April Blair

Director:
Patricia Riggen

Stars:
Bridgit Mendler, Hayley Kiyoko, Naomi Scott, Blake Michael

Broadcast:
Apr 15, 2011, Disney Channel

Length:
103 min (Original), 113 min (Extended)

DVD:
2011 Extended Edition

Digital:
Amazon, iTunes, Netflix

Soundtrack:
2011 (CD)

Phineas and Ferb the Movie: Across the 2nd Dimension (2011)

Disney Channel Original Movie

Source:
Spin-off from *Phineas and Ferb* (2007-2015) Disney Channel TV series

Writers:
Jon Colton Barry, Dan Povenmire, Jeff 'Swampy' Marsh

Directors:
Robert Hughes, Dan Povenmire

Broadcast:
Aug 5, 2011, Disney Channel

Length:
78 min

Movie:
Phineas and Ferb the Movie: Across the 2nd Dimension (2011, Spain)

Video Game:
Phineas and Ferb: Across the 2nd Dimension (2011) Wii, PS3, DS

DVD:
2011, 2015

Digital:
Amazon, iTunes, Netflix

Soundtrack:
2011 (CD)

Geek Charming (2011)

Disney Channel Original Movie

Source:
Geek Charming (2009) Robin Palmer

Writers:
Elizabeth Hackett, Hilary Galanoy

Director:
Jeffrey Hornaday

Stars:
Sarah Hyland, Matt Prokop, Jordan Nichols, Sasha Pieterse

Broadcast:
Nov 11, 2011, Disney Channel

Length:
97 min

DVD:
2012

Digital:
Amazon, iTunes

Good Luck Charlie, It's Christmas! (2011)

Disney Channel Original Movie

Source:
Spin-off from *Good Luck Charlie* (2010-2014) Disney Channel TV series

Writers:
Geoff Rodkey

Director:
Arlene Sanford

Stars:
Bridgit Mendler, Leigh-Allyn Baker, Bradley Steven Perry, Mia Talerico

Broadcast:
Dec 2, 2011, Disney Channel

Length:
80 min

DVD:
2012

Digital:
iTunes, Netflix

Frenemies (2012)

Disney Channel Original Movie

Source:
Frenemies (2008) Alexa Young

Writers:
James Krieg, Dava Savel (story/screenplay), Wendy Weiner (screenplay)

Director:
Daisy von Scherler Mayer

Stars:
Bella Thorne, Zendaya, Stefanie Scott, Nick Robinson

Broadcast:
Jan 13, 2012, Disney Channel

Length:
87 min

Digital:
iTunes, Netflix

Radio Rebel (2012)
Disney Channel Original Movie

Source:
Shrinking Violet (2009) Danielle Joseph

Writers:
Erik Patterson, Jessica Scott

Director:
Peter Howitt

Stars:
Debby Ryan, Sarena Parmar, Adam DiMarco, Merritt Patterson

Broadcast:
Feb 17, 2012, Disney Channel

Length:
85 min

DVD:
2012 (Image Entertainment), 2014 Debby Ryan Double Feature (Image Entertainment)

Digital:
Amazon, iTunes, Vudu

Soundtrack:
2012 (CD)

Let It Shine (2012)
Disney Channel Original Movie

Writers:
Eric Daniel (story/screenplay), Don D. Scott (screenplay)

Director:
Paul Hoen

Stars:
Tyler James Williams, Coco Jones, Trevor Jackson, Brandon Mychal Smith

Broadcast:
Jun 15, 2012, Disney Channel

Length:
104 min (Extended)

DVD:
2012 Extended Edition

Digital:
iTunes, Netflix

Soundtrack:
2012 (CD)

Girl vs. Monster (2012)

Disney Channel Original Movie

Writers:
Annie DeYoung (story/screenplay), Ron McGee (screenplay)

Director:
Stuart Gillard

Stars:
Olivia Holt, Brendan Meyer, Kerris Dorsey, Katherine McNamara

Broadcast:
Oct 12, 2012, Disney Channel

Length:
89 min

Digital:
Amazon, iTunes, Netflix

Teen Beach Movie (2013)

Disney Channel Original Movie

Writers:
Vince Marcello, Mark Landry (story/screenplay), Robert Horn (screenplay)

Director:
Jeffrey Hornaday

Stars:
Ross Lynch, Mala Mitchell, Grace Phipps, Garrett Clayton

Broadcast:
Jul 19, 2013, Disney Channel

Length:
95 min

TV Movie:
Teen Beach 2 (2015) Sequel
DVD:
2013
Digital:
Amazon, iTunes
Soundtrack:
2013 (CD)

Cloud 9 (2014)
Disney Channel Original Movie
Writers:
Justin Ware
Director:
Paul Hoen
Stars:
Luke Benward, Dove Cameron, Kiersey Clemons, Mike C. Manning
Broadcast:
Jan 17, 2014, Disney Channel
Length:
87 min
DVD:
2014
Digital:
Amazon, iTunes

Zapped (2014)
Disney Channel Original Movie
Source:
Boys Are Dogs (2008) Leslie Margolis
Writers:
Rachelle Skoretz (story), Billy Eddy, Matt Eddy (screenplay)
Director:
Peter DeLuise
Stars:
Zendaya, Chanelle Peloso, Spencer Boldman, Emilia McCarthy
Broadcast:
Jun 27, 2014, Disney Channel

Length:
92 min
DVD:
2015
Digital:
Amazon, iTunes, Vudu

How to Build a Better Boy (2014)

Disney Channel Original Movie

Writers:
Jason Mayland
Director:
Paul Hoen
Stars:
Kelli Berglund, China Ann McClain, Marshall Williams, Roger Bart
Broadcast:
Aug 15, 2014, Disney Channel
Length:
92 min
Digital:
Amazon, iTunes

Bad Hair Day (2015)

Disney Channel Original Movie

Writers:
Eric Gardner, Steven H. Wilson (story/screenplay), Matt Eddy, Billy Eddy (screenplay)
Director:
Erik Canuel
Stars:
Laura Marano, Leigh-Allyn Baker, Christian Campbell, Alain Goulem
Broadcast:
Feb 13, 2015, Disney Channel
Length:
91 min
Digital:
Amazon, iTunes

Teen Beach 2 (2015)

Disney Channel Original Movie

Source:
Sequel to *Teen Beach Movie* (2013) TV movie

Writers:
Dan Berendesen, Robert Horn (story), Matt Eddy, Billy Eddy (screenplay)

Director:
Jeffrey Hornaday

Stars:
Ross Lynch, Maia Mitchell, Grace Phipps, Garrett Clayton

Broadcast:
Jun 26, 2015, Disney Channel

Length:
104 min

DVD:
2015

Digital:
Amazon, iTunes

Soundtrack:
2015 (CD)

Descendants (2015)

Disney Channel Original Movie

Source:
Characters drawn from various animated Disney films

Writers:
Josann McGibbon

Director:
Kenny Ortega

Stars:
Dove Cameron, Cameron Boyce, Booboo Stewart, Sofia Carson

Broadcast:
Jul 31, 2015, Disney Channel

Length:
112 min

Comic Books:
- *Disney Manga: Descendants: Rotten to the Core* (#1-3, 2017) [Collection: *The Rotten to the Core Trilogy: The Complete Collection*

(2018)]

- *Disney Manga: Descendants: Evie's Wicked Runaway* (#1-3, 2018)

TV Series:
- *Descendants: Wicked World* (2015-2017) Animated Disney Channel sequel [Collection: Amazon]
- *Descendants: School of Secrets* (2015) Watch Disney Channel spin-off

TV Movie:
- *Descendants 2* (2017) Sequel
- *Descendants 3* (2019) Sequel

DVD:
2015

Digital:
Amazon, iTunes

Soundtrack:
2015 (CD)

Invisible Sister (2015)

Disney Channel Original Movie

Source:
My Invisible Sister (2010) Beatrice Colin, Sara Pinto

Writers:
Amy Rardin, Jessica O'Toole (story), Billy Eddy, Matt Eddy (story/screenplay)

Director:
Paul Hoen

Stars:
Rowan Blanchard, Paris Berelc, Karan Barr, Rachel Crow

Broadcast:
Oct 9, 2015, Disney Channel

Length:
77 min

Digital:
Amazon, iTunes

The Lion Guard: Return of the Roar (2015)

Disney Channel Original Movie

Source:
Spin-off from *The Lion King* (1994)

Writers:
Ford Riley

Director:
Howry Parkins

Broadcast:
Nov 22, 2015, Disney Channel

Length:
44 min

TV Series:
The Lion Guard (2016+) Disney Junior

DVD:
2016

Digital:
Amazon, iTunes

Soundtrack:
2016 (CD)

Adventures in Babysitting (2016)

Disney Channel Original Movie

Source:
Remake of *Adventures in Babysitting* (Touchstone, 1987)

Writers:
Tiffany Paulsen

Director:
John Schultz

Stars:
Sabrina Carpenter, Sofia Carson, Nikki Hahn, Max Gecowets

Broadcast:
Jun 24, 2016, Disney Channel

Length:
93 min

DVD:
2016

Digital:
Amazon, iTunes

The Swap (2016)

Disney Channel Original Movie

Source:
The Swap (2014) Megan Shull

Writers:
Charlie Shahnaian, Shari Simpson

Director:
Jay Karas

Stars:
Peyton List, Jacob Bertrand, Claire Rankin, Darrin Rose

Broadcast:
Oct 7, 2016, Disney Channel

Length:
89 min

DVD:
2018 (Monarch Home Video)

Digital:
Amazon, iTunes, Vudu

Tangled: Before Ever After (2017)

Disney Channel Original Movie

AKA:
Tangled Before Ever After

Source:
Sequel to *Tangled* (2010)

Writers:
Jase Ricci

Directors:
Tom Caulfield, Stephen Sandoval

Broadcast:
Mar 10, 2017, Disney Channel

Length:
55 min

TV Series:
Tangled: The Series (2017+) Disney Channel sequel

DVD:
2017

Digital:
Amazon, iTunes

Descendants 2 (2017)

Disney Channel Original Movie

Source:
Sequel to *Descendants* (2015) TV movie

Writers:
Sara Parriott, Josann McGibbon

Director:
Kenny Ortega

Stars:
Dove Cameron, Cameron Boyce, Sofia Carson, Booboo Stewart

Broadcast:
Jul 21, 2017, Disney Channel

Length:
111 min

DVD:
2017

Digital:
Amazon, iTunes

Soundtrack:
2017 (CD)

Zombies (2018)

Disney Channel Original Movie

AKA:
Z-O-M-B-I-E-S

Source:
Zombies and Cheerleaders (2012) Unaired Disney Channel TV pilot

Writers:
David Light, Joseph Raso

Director:
Paul Hoen

Stars:
Milo Manheim, Meg Donnelly, Trevor Tordjman, Kylee Russell

Broadcast:
Feb 16, 2018

Length:
94 min

DVD:
2018

Digital:
Amazon, Vudu

Soundtrack:
2018 (CD)

Freaky Friday (2018)
Disney Channel Original Movie

Source:
Freaky Friday (2016+) Stage musical

Writers:
Bridget Carpenter, Brian Yorkey

Director:
Steve Carr

Stars:
Cozi Zuehlsdorff, Heidi Blickenstaff, Ricky He, Alex Désert

Broadcast:
Aug 10, 2018, Disney Channel

Length:
90 min

DVD:
2018

Soundtrack:
2018 (CD)

Kim Possible (2019)
Disney Channel Original Movie

Source:
Live-action remake of *Kim Possible* (2002-2007) TV series

Writers:
Josh A Cagan, Mark McCorkle, Robert Schooley

Directors:
Zack Lipovsky, Adam B. Stein

Stars:
Sadie Stanley, Sean Giambrone, Ciara Riley Wilson, Todd Stashwick

Broadcast:
Feb 15, 2019, Disney Channel

Length:
90 min

DVD:
2019

Disney's television movie releases are set to continue with *Descendants 3* on the Disney Channel in 2019. Several movies have also been announced for the new Disney+ streaming service (which had not launched at time of writing). A question remains about whether movies released direct to streaming are the equivalent of direct-to-video movies or TV movies, and thus which volume these titles should appear in. Since Volume 1 is already published, I have opted to include details of upcoming Disney+ movies here in Volume 2. Information about these upcoming movies is limited and liable to change, but the following are in production and due to hit a Disney home entertainment platform soon:

Dolphin Reef

Disneynature

Writers:
David Fowler

Director:
Keith Scholey

Narrator:
Natalie Portman

Noelle

Writers:
Marc Lawrence

Director:
Marc Lawrence

Stars:
Anna Kendrick, Bill Hader, Shirley MacLaine

Lady and the Tramp (2019)

Source:
Remake of *Lady and the Tramp* (1955)

Writers:
Andrew Bujalski

Director:
Charlie Bean

Voices:
Tessa Thompson, Justin Theroux, Sam Elliott, Ashley Jensen

Magic Camp

Writers:
Micah Fitzerman-Blue, Noah Harpster, Matt Spicer, Max Winkler, Dan Gregor, Doug Mand

Director:
Marc Waters

Stars:
Gillian Jacobs, Josie Totah, Adam Devine, Aldis Hodge

Stargirl (2020)

Source:
Stargirl (2000) Jerry Spinelli

Writers:
Kristin Hahn, Jordan Horowitz, Jerry Spinelli

Director:
Julia Hart

Stars:
Darby Stanchfield, Giancarlo Esposito, Maximiliano Hernández, Karan Brar

Timmy Failure

Source:
Timmy Failure books (2013-2018) Stephan Pastis

Writers:
Stephan Pastis, Tom McCarthy

Director:
Tom McCarthy

Stars:
Winslow Fegley, Ophelia Lovibond

Togo

Writers:
Tom Flynn

Director:
Ericson Core

Stars:
Willem Dafoe, Christopher Heyerdahl, Michael McElhatton, Jamie McShane

The following movies have also been announced:

The Sword in the Stone

Source:
Remake of *The Sword in the Stone* (1973)

Writers:
Bryan Cogman

Director:
Juan Carlos Fresnadillo

Phineas and Ferb (2020)

Source:
Spin-off from *Phineas and Ferb* (2007-2015) Disney Channel TV series

Sister Act 3

Source:
Second sequel to *Sister Act* (1992) Touchstone movie

The Mighty Ducks

Source:
Remake of *The Mighty Ducks* (1992)

CHECKLIST 1

TV Movies

The following checklist of Disney TV movies broadcast between 1959 and 2019 serves as an index of sorts to help you locate the entries within the book when you don't know what year they were broadcast. It also doubles as a checklist to keep track of the movies you've seen or own. Entries marked with an x and a number indicates that the movie was originally broadcast in 2 or more parts. E.g. '*Moochie of the Little League* (1959) x2' means that this movie was originally broadcast in two parts on an anthology series. Anthology episodes that were not feature-length or multi-part movies can be found on Checklist 2.

A

- ❑ The Absent-Minded Professor (1988)
- ❑ The Absent-Minded Professor: Trading Places (1989)
- ❑ Adventures in Babysitting (2016)
- ❑ Alley Cats Strike! (2000)
- ❑ Angels in the Endzone (1997)
- ❑ Angels in the Infield (2000)
- ❑ Anne of Avonlea: The Continuing Story of Anne of Green Gables (1987) x4
- ❑ Annie (1999)
- ❑ Atta Girl, Kelly! (1967) x3
- ❑ Avalon High (2010)

B

- ❑ Back Home (1990)
- ❑ Back to Hannibal: The Return of Tom Sawyer and Huckleberry Finn (1990)
- ❑ Bad Hair Day (2015)
- ❑ Bailey's Mistake (2001)
- ❑ The Ballad of Hector the Stowaway Dog (1964) x2
- ❑ Ballerina (1966) x2
- ❑ Balloon Farm (1999)

- ❑ The Barefoot Executive (1995)
- ❑ Barry of the Great St. Bernard (1977) x2
- ❑ Bayou Boy (1971) x2
- ❑ Bejewelled (1991)
- ❑ Beverly Hills Family Robinson (1997)
- ❑ Bigfoot (1987)
- ❑ Black Arrow (1985)
- ❑ The Blue Yonder (1985)
- ❑ Boomerang, Dog of Many Talents (1968) x2
- ❑ Born to Run (1979) x2
- ❑ The Boy and the Bronc Buster (1973) x2
- ❑ A Boy Called Nuthin' (1967) x2
- ❑ The Boy Who Talked to Badgers (1975) x2
- ❑ The Boy Who Stole the Elephant (1970) x2
- ❑ The B.R.A.T. Patrol (1986)
- ❑ Brian's Song (2001)
- ❑ Bride of Boogedy (1987)
- ❑ Brink! (1998)
- ❑ Bristle Face (1964) x2
- ❑ Buffalo Dreams (2005)

C

- ❑ Cadet Kelly (2002)
- ❑ Camp Rock (2008)
- ❑ Camp Rock 2: The Final Jam (2010)
- ❑ Can of Worms (1999)
- ❑ Chandar, the Black Leopard of Ceylon (1972) x2
- ❑ The Cheetah Girls (2003)
- ❑ The Cheetah Girls: One World (2008)
- ❑ The Cheetah Girls 2 (2006)
- ❑ Child of Glass (1978)
- ❑ Child Star: The Shirley Temple Story (2001)
- ❑ Chip 'n Dale's Rescue Rangers to the Rescue (1989)
- ❑ Chips, the War Dog (1990)
- ❑ The Christmas Star (1986)
- ❑ The Christmas Tree (1996)
- ❑ The Christmas Visitor (1987)
- ❑ Cloud 9 (2014)
- ❑ The Color of Friendship (2000)
- ❑ The Computer Wore Tennis Shoes (1995)
- ❑ Cow Belles (2006)

D

- ❏ Dadnapped (2009)
- ❏ Danny, the Champion of the World (1989)
- ❏ Day-O (1992)
- ❏ Den Brother (2010)
- ❏ Descendants (2015)
- ❏ Descendants 2 (2017)
- ❏ Diamonds on Wheels (1974) x3
- ❏ Donovan's Kid (1979) x2
- ❏ Don't Look Under the Bed (1999)
- ❏ Double Agent (1987)
- ❏ Double Switch (1987)
- ❏ Double Teamed (2002)
- ❏ Down the Long Hills (1986)
- ❏ DuckTales: Time is Money (1988)
- ❏ DuckTales: Treasure of the Golden Suns (1987)

E

- ❏ Earth*Star Voyager (1988)
- ❏ Eddie's Million Dollar Cook-Off (2003)
- ❏ Eloise at Christmastime (2003)
- ❏ Eloise at the Plaza (2003)
- ❏ Encino Woman (1996)
- ❏ The Ernest Green Story (1993)
- ❏ Escapade in Florence (1962) x2
- ❏ Escape to Witch Mountain (1995)
- ❏ The Even Stevens Movie (2003)
- ❏ Exile (1990)

F

- ❏ The Facts of Life Reunion (2001)
- ❏ A Fighting Choice
- ❏ Flash (1997)
- ❏ The Flight of the Grey Wolf (1976) x2
- ❏ For the Love of Willadean (1964) x2
- ❏ The Four Diamonds (1995)
- ❏ 14 Going on 30 (1988)
- ❏ Freaky Friday (1995)
- ❏ Freaky Friday (2018)
- ❏ Frenemies (2012)
- ❏ A Friendship in Vienna (1988)
- ❏ Full-Court Miracle (2003)
- ❏ The Further Adventures of Gallegher (1965) x3

G

- ❑ Gallegher (1965) x3
- ❑ Gallegher Goes West (1966-1967) x4
- ❑ The Garbage Picking Field Goal Kicking Philadelphia Phenomenon (1998)
- ❑ Geek Charming (2011)
- ❑ Genius (1999)
- ❑ Geppetto (2000)
- ❑ Get a Clue (2002)
- ❑ The Ghost of Cypress Swamp (1977)
- ❑ The Ghosts of Buxley Hall (1980-1981) x2
- ❑ Girl Vs. Monster (2012)
- ❑ The Girl Who Spelled Freedom (1986)
- ❑ Go Figure (2005)
- ❑ Going to the Mat (2004)
- ❑ Goldrush: A Real Life Alaskan Adventure (1998)
- ❑ Gone are the Dayes (1984)
- ❑ Goodbye, Miss 4, of July (1988)
- ❑ Good Luck Charlie, It's Christmas! (2011)
- ❑ Good Old Boy (1988)
- ❑ Gotta Kick It Up! (2002)
- ❑ Great Expectations (1989) x2

H

- ❑ Hacksaw (1971) x2
- ❑ Halloweentown (1998)
- ❑ Halloweentown II: Kalabar's Revenge (2001)
- ❑ Halloweentown High (2004)
- ❑ Hamad and the Pirates (1971) x2
- ❑ Hans Brinker, or the Silver Skates (1962) x2
- ❑ Harriet the Spy: Blog Wars (2010)
- ❑ Hatching Pete (2009)
- ❑ H-E Double Hockey Sticks (1999)
- ❑ Heidi (1993)
- ❑ Help Wanted: Kids (1986)
- ❑ Hero in the Family (1986)
- ❑ The High Flying Spy (1972) x3
- ❑ High School Musical (2006)
- ❑ High School Musical 2 (2007)
- ❑ Hog Wild (1974) x2
- ❑ The Horsemasters (1961) x2
- ❑ Horse Sense (1999)
- ❑ The Horse Without a Head (1963) x2

- ❑ Hounded (2001)
- ❑ How to Build a Better Boy (2014)

I

- ❑ I-Man (1986)
- ❑ In the Nick of Time (1991)
- ❑ Invisible Sister (2015)

J

- ❑ The Jennie Project (2001)
- ❑ Jett Jackson: The Movie (2001)
- ❑ Johnny Kapahala: Back on Board (2007)
- ❑ Johnny Shiloh (1963) x2
- ❑ Johnny Tsunami (1999)
- ❑ Jump In! (2007)
- ❑ Jumping Ship (2001)
- ❑ Justin Case (1988)
- ❑ Justin Morgan Had a Horse (1972) x2

K

- ❑ The Kids Who Knew Too Much (1980)
- ❑ Kilroy (1965) x 4
- ❑ Kim Possible (2019)
- ❑ Kim Possible: A Sitch in Time (2003)
- ❑ Kim Possible: So the Drama (2005)
- ❑ Kit Carson and the Mountain Men (1977) x2
- ❑ A Knight in Camelot (1998)

L

- ❑ Ladies and the Champ (2001)
- ❑ Lantern Hill (1990)
- ❑ The Leftovers (1986)
- ❑ Lefty, the Dingaling Lynx (1971) x2
- ❑ The Legend of Young Dick Turpin (1966) x2
- ❑ Lemonade Mouth (2011)
- ❑ Leroy & Stitch (2006)
- ❑ Let It Shine (2012)
- ❑ The Liberators (1987)
- ❑ Life is Ruff (2005)
- ❑ Life-Size (2000)
- ❑ The Lion Guard: Return of the Roar (2015)
- ❑ The Little Kidnappers (1990)

- ❑ The Little Riders (1995)
- ❑ Little Spies (1986)
- ❑ Looking for Miracles (1989)
- ❑ The Loretta Claiborne Story (2000)
- ❑ Lots of Luck (1985)
- ❑ The Love Bug (1997)
- ❑ Love Leads the Way (1984)
- ❑ The Luck of the Irish (2001)

M

- ❑ The Magnificent Rebel (1962) x2
- ❑ Mail to the Chief (2000)
- ❑ Mark Twain and Me (1991)
- ❑ Meet the Munceys (1988)
- ❑ Menace on the Mountain (1970) x2
- ❑ Michael O'Hara the Fourth (1972) x2
- ❑ The Million Dollar Dixie Deliverance (1978)
- ❑ Minute Men (2008)
- ❑ Miracle at Midnight (1998)
- ❑ Miracle Child (1993)
- ❑ Miracle in Lane 2 (2000)
- ❑ The Miracle Worker (2000)
- ❑ Mr. Headmistress (1998)
- ❑ Model Behavior (2000)
- ❑ A Mom for Christmas (1990)
- ❑ Mom's Got a Date with a Vampire (2000)
- ❑ Moochie of Pop Warner Football (1960) x2
- ❑ Moochie of the Little League (1959) x2
- ❑ The Mooncussers (1962) x2
- ❑ Mother Goose Rock 'n' Rhyme (1990)
- ❑ A Mother's Courage: The Mary Thomas Story (1989)
- ❑ Motocrossed (2001)
- ❑ A Muppets Christmas: Letters to Santa (2008)
- ❑ The Muppets' Wizard of Oz (2005)
- ❑ Murder She Purred: A Mrs. Murphy Mystery (1998)
- ❑ The Music Man (2003)
- ❑ Mustang! (1973) x2
- ❑ My Date with the President's Daughter (1998)
- ❑ My Dog, the Thief (1969) x2
- ❑ The Mystery in Dracula's Castle (1973) x2
- ❑ The Mystery of Edward Sims (1968) x2

N

- ❏ The New Adventures of Spin and Marty: Suspect Behavior (2000)
- ❏ The New Swiss Family Robinson (1999)
- ❏ Nightjohn (1995)
- ❏ The Night Train to Kathmandu (1988)
- ❏ Noah (1998)
- ❏ Northern Lights (1997)
- ❏ Not Quite Human (1987)
- ❏ Not Quite Human II (1989)
- ❏ Now You See It... (2005)

O

- ❏ The Old Curiosity Shop (1995) x2
- ❏ Oliver Twist (1997)
- ❏ Ollie Hopnoodle's Haven of Bliss (1988)
- ❏ The Omega Connection (1979)
- ❏ Once Upon a Mattress (2005)
- ❏ The 100 Lives of Black Jack Savage (1991)
- ❏ One More Mountain (1994)
- ❏ On Promised Land (1994)
- ❏ The Other Me (2000)

P

- ❏ Pablo and the Dancing Chihuahua (1968) x2
- ❏ The Parent Trap II (1986)
- ❏ The Parent Trap III (1989)
- ❏ The Parent Trap IV: Hawaiian Honeymoon (1989) x2
- ❏ Perfect Harmony (1991)
- ❏ Phantom of the Megaplex (2000)
- ❏ Phenomenon II (2003)
- ❏ Phineas and Ferb the Movie: Across the 2, Dimension (2011)
- ❏ Pixel Perfect (2004)
- ❏ Polly (1989)
- ❏ Polly: Comin' Home! (1990)
- ❏ The Pooch and the Pauper (2000)
- ❏ The Poof Point (2001)
- ❏ The Prince and the Pauper (1962) x3
- ❏ Princess of Thieves (2001)
- ❏ Princess Protection Program (2009)
- ❏ Principal Takes a Holiday (1998)
- ❏ The Proud Family Movie (2005)
- ❏ P.U.N.K.S. (1999)

Q

❑ Quints (2000)

R

❑ Radio Rebel (2012)
❑ Read It and Weep (2006)
❑ Ready to Run (2000)
❑ Return of the Big Cat (1974) x2
❑ The Return of the Shaggy Dog (1987)
❑ Return to Halloweentown (2006)
❑ The Richest Cat in the World (1986)
❑ Ride a Northbound Horse (1969) x2
❑ Right on Track (2003)
❑ A Ring of Endless Light (2002)
❑ Rip Girls (2000)
❑ Rock 'n' Roll Mom (1988)
❑ Rodgers & Hammerstein's Cinderella (1997)
❑ Ruby Bridges (1998)

S

❑ Safety Patrol (1998)
❑ A Saintly Switch (1999)
❑ Sammy, the Way-Out Seal (1962) x2
❑ Sancho, the Homing Steer (1962) x2
❑ Santa Who? (2000)
❑ Save the Dog! (1988)
❑ The Scarecrow of Romney Marsh (1964) x3
❑ The Scream Team (2002)
❑ The Secret of Boyne Castle (1969) x3
❑ The Secret of Lost Valley (1980) x2
❑ The Secret of the Pond (1975) x2
❑ Secrets of the Pirates' Inn (1969) x2
❑ Selma, Lord, Selma (1999)
❑ Shadow of Fear (1979) x2
❑ The Shaggy Dog (1994)
❑ She Stood Alone (1991)
❑ 16 Wishes (2010)
❑ Sky High (1990) x2
❑ The Sky's the Limit (1975) x2
❑ The Sky Trap (1979)
❑ Smart House (1999)
❑ Smoke (1970) x2

- ❑ Snow Bear (1970) x2
- ❑ Sounder (2003)
- ❑ Spies (1993)
- ❑ Splash, Too (1988)
- ❑ Spooner (1989)
- ❑ Spot Marks the X (1986)
- ❑ StarStruck (2010)
- ❑ Stepsister from Planet Weird (2000)
- ❑ Still Not Quite Human (1992)
- ❑ Strange Companions (1987)
- ❑ The Strange Monster of Strawberry Cove (1971) x2
- ❑ Stuck in the Suburbs (2004)
- ❑ Student Exchange (1987)
- ❑ The Suite Life Movie (2011)
- ❑ The Sultan and the Rock Star (1980)
- ❑ Sunday Drive (1986)
- ❑ Super DuckTales (1989)
- ❑ The Swap (2016)

T

- ❑ TaleSpin: Plunder & Lightning (1990)
- ❑ Tangled: Before Ever After (2017)
- ❑ Teen Beach Movie (2013)
- ❑ Teen Beach 2 (2015)
- ❑ The Tenderfoot (1964) x3
- ❑ The Thanksgiving Promise (1986)
- ❑ The Thirteenth Year (1999)
- ❑ Three Without Fear (1971) x2
- ❑ Tiger Cruise (2004)
- ❑ Tiger Town (1983)
- ❑ Toothless (1997)
- ❑ Tourist Trap (1998)
- ❑ Tower of Terror (1997)
- ❑ The Track of the African Bongo (1977) x2
- ❑ Trail of Danger (1978) x2
- ❑ The Treasure of San Bosco Reef (1968) x2
- ❑ Tru Confessions (2002)
- ❑ 'Twas the Night (2001)
- ❑ Twitches (2005)
- ❑ Twitches Too (2007)

U

❏ The Ultimate Christmas Present (2000)
❏ The Undergrads (1985)
❏ Under Wraps (1997)
❏ Up, Up, and Away (2000)

W

❏ The Wacky Zoo of Morgan City (1970) x2
❏ Waco & Rhinehart (1987)
❏ Walt: The Man Behind the Myth (2001)
❏ The Waltz King (1963) x2
❏ Way Down Cellar (1968) x2
❏ Wendy Wu: Homecoming Warrior (2006)
❏ The Whipping Boy (1994)
❏ The Whiz Kid and the Carnival Caper (1976) x2
❏ The Whiz Kid and the Mystery at Riverton (1974) x2
❏ Willie and the Yank (1967) x3
❏ Wizards of Waverly Place: The Movie (2009)
❏ A Wrinkle in Time (2003)

Y

❏ You Lucky Dog (1998)
❏ Young Again (1986)
❏ Young Harry Houdini (1987)
❏ The Young Loner (1968) x2
❏ The Young Runaways (1978)
❏ You Ruined My Life (1987)
❏ You Wish! (2003)

Z

❏ Zapped (2014)
❏ Zenon: Girl of the 21, Century (1999)
❏ Zenon: The Zequel (2001)
❏ Zenon: Z3 (2004)
❏ Zombies

CHECKLIST 2

Anthology Episodes

While Checklist 1 features multi-part or feature-length movies, Checklist 2 covers the other entries found in this volume, namely episodes of the *Disneyland* anthology show and its successors. These might be compilations of cartoons, behind the scenes documentaries, or episodes in mini-series such as Davy Crockett or Elfego Baca. These individual episodes span the first Disney TV special *One Hour in Disneyland* (1950) and the first series of *Disneyland* in 1954 up to *The Magical World of Disney* in 1990. Mickey Mouse Club serials are included with the identifier 'MMC'.

A

- ☐ Adios El Cuchillo (1960)
- ☐ Adventure in Dairyland (1956-1957) MMC
- ☐ Adventure in Wildwood Heart (1957)
- ☐ The Adventure Story (1957)
- ☐ An Adventure in Art (1958)
- ☐ An Adventure in Color (1961)
- ☐ Adventure in Satan's Canyon (1974)
- ☐ Adventures in Fantasy (1957)
- ☐ An Adventure in the Magic Kingdom (1958)
- ☐ The Adventures of Chip 'n' Dale (1959)
- ☐ The Adventures of Clint and Mac (1957-1958) MMC
- ☐ The Adventures of Mickey Mouse (1955)
- ☐ The Adventures of Pollyanna (1982)
- ☐ The Adventures of Spin and Marty (1955-1956) MMC
- ☐ All About Magic (1957)
- ☐ Along the Oregon Trail (1956)
- ☐ Ambush at Laredo (1958)
- ☐ And Chase the Buffalo (1960)
- ☐ Annette (1957-1958) MMC
- ☐ Antarctica: Operation Deep Freeze (1957)

❏ Antarctica—Past and Present (1956)
❏ Apache Friendship (1960)
❏ Ask Max (1986)
❏ At Home with Donald Duck (1956)
❏ Attorney at Law (1959)
❏ Auld Acquaintance (1961)

B

❏ Backstage Party (1961)
❏ Baseball Fever (1979)
❏ Battle for Survival (1961)
❏ Behind the Cameras at Lapland (1956)
❏ Behind the Scenes with Fess Parker (1956)
❏ Behind the True-Life Cameras (1955)
❏ The Best Doggoned Dog in the World (1957)
❏ Beyond Witch Mountain (1982)
❏ The Birth of the Swamp Fox (1959)
❏ The Bluegrass Special (1977)
❏ Border Collie (1955-1956) MMC
❏ The Boys of the Western Sea (1956-1957) MMC
❏ The Boy Who Flew with Condors (1967)
❏ Brand New Life: Above and Beyond Therapy (1989)
❏ Brand New Life: Children of a Legal Mom (1990)
❏ Brand New Life: I Fought the Law (1989)
❏ Brand New Life: Private School (1989)
❏ Brimstone, the Amish Horse (1968)
❏ Brother Against Brother (1959)

C

❏ Call It Courage (1973)
❏ Cameras in Africa (1954)
❏ Cameras in Samoa (1956)
❏ Carlo, the Sierra Coyote (1974)
❏ Carnival Time (1962)
❏ Casebusters (1986)
❏ A Case of Treason (1960)
❏ Cavalcade of Songs (1955)
❏ Chango, Guardian of the Mayan Treasure (1972)
❏ Charlie Crowfoot and the Coati Mundi (1971)
❏ The Cherokee Trail (1981)
❏ Chester, Yesterday's Horse (1973)
❏ Chico, the Misunderstood Coyote (1961)

- ❏ Christmas at Walt Disney World (1978)
- ❏ The City Fox (1972)
- ❏ Concho, the Coyote Who Wasn't (1966)
- ❏ Corky and White Shadow (1955-1956) MMC
- ❏ The Coyote's Lament (1961)
- ❏ The Crisler Story (1957)
- ❏ Cristobalito, the Calypso Colt (1970)

D

- ❏ Dateline: Disneyland (1955)
- ❏ Davy Crockett: A Letter to Polly (1989)
- ❏ Davy Crockett: A Natural Man (1988)
- ❏ Davy Crockett and the River Pirates (1955)
- ❏ Davy Crockett at the Alamo (1955)
- ❏ Davy Crockett Goes to Congress (1955)
- ❏ Davy Crockett: Guardian Spirit (1989)
- ❏ Davy Crockett: Indian Fighter (1954)
- ❏ Davy Crockett: Rainbow in the Thunder (1988)
- ❏ Davy Crockett's Keelboat Race (1955)
- ❏ Davy Crockett: A Warrior's Farewell (1989)
- ❏ A Day in the Life of Donald Duck (1956)
- ❏ Day of Reckoning (1960)
- ❏ The Deacon Street Deer (1986)
- ❏ Deacon, the High Noon Dog (1975)
- ❏ Desperado from Tombstone (1960)
- ❏ Disney Animation: The Illusion of Life (1981)
- ❏ A Disney Christmas Gift (1982)
- ❏ Disney Goes to the Oscars (1986)
- ❏ Disneyland After Dark (1962)
- ❏ Disneyland Around the Seasons (1966)
- ❏ Disneyland '59 (1959)
- ❏ Disneyland Goes to the World's Fair (1964)
- ❏ Disneyland's All-Star Comedy Circus (1988)
- ❏ Disneyland's 35, Anniversary Celebration (1990)
- ❏ Disneyland Showtime (1970)
- ❏ The Disneyland Story (1954)
- ❏ Disneyland 10, Anniversary (1965)
- ❏ Disneyland, the Park (1957)
- ❏ The Disney-MGM Studios Theme Park Grand Opening (1989)
- ❏ Disney on Parade (1971)
- ❏ Disney's All-American Sports Nuts (1988)
- ❏ Disney's Fluppy Dogs (1986)
- ❏ Disney's Greatest Dog Stars (1976)

- ❏ Disney's Halloween Treat (1982)
- ❏ Disney's Oscar Winners (1980)
- ❏ The Donald Duck Story (1954)
- ❏ Donald's Award (1957)
- ❏ Donald's Silver Anniversary (1960)
- ❏ Donald's Valentine's Day Salute (1980)
- ❏ Donald's Weekend (1958)
- ❏ Duck Flies Coop (1959)
- ❏ Duck for Hire (1957)
- ❏ A DuckTales Valentine (1990)

E

- ❏ El Bandido (1960)
- ❏ Emerald Cove (1993) MMC
- ❏ End of the Trail (1961)
- ❏ EPCOT Center: The Opening Celebration (1982)
- ❏ Escape to Paradise (1960)

F

- ❏ Fantasy on Skis (1962)
- ❏ Faraway Places: High, Hot and Wet (1958)
- ❏ The Feather Farm (1969)
- ❏ 50 Happy Years (1973)
- ❏ A Fire Called Jeremiah (1961)
- ❏ Fire on Kelly Mountain (1973)
- ❏ The First Americans (1956-1957) MMC
- ❏ Flash, the Teenage Otter (1961)
- ❏ Fly with Von Drake (1963)
- ❏ The Footloose Goose (1975)
- ❏ Four Down and Five Lives to Go (1958)
- ❏ Four Fabulous Characters (1957)
- ❏ Four Tales on a Mouse (1958)
- ❏ The Fourth Anniversary Show (1957)
- ❏ Frank Clell's in Town (1961)
- ❏ Friendly Enemies at War (1960)
- ❏ From All of Us, to All of You (1958)
- ❏ From Aesop to Hans Christian Andersen (1955)
- ❏ From the Pirates of the Caribbean to the World of Tomorrow (1968)
- ❏ The Further Adventures of Spin and Marty (1956-1957) MMC
- ❏ A Further Report on Disneyland (1955)
- ❏ Fuzzbucket (1986)

G

- ❑ Geronimo's Revenge (1960)
- ❑ The Golden Horseshoe Revue (1962)
- ❑ The Goofy Sports Story (1956)
- ❑ The Goofy Success Story (1955)
- ❑ Goofy's Cavalcade of Sports (1956)
- ❑ The Golden Dog (1977)
- ❑ Go West, Young Dog (1977)
- ❑ The Great Cat Family (1956)
- ❑ Great Moments in Disney Animation (1987)
- ❑ Greta, the Misfit Greyhound (1963)
- ❑ The Griswold Murder (1959)
- ❑ Gun Shy (1983) x6
- ❑ Gus Tomlin is Dead (1960)

H

- ❑ Halloween Hall o' Fame (1977)
- ❑ The Hardy Boys: The Mystery of Ghost Farm (1957-1958) MMC
- ❑ The Hardy Boys: The Mystery of the Applegate Treasure (1956-1957) MMC
- ❑ Herbie, the Love Bug (1982) x5
- ❑ Highway to Trouble (1959)
- ❑ Holiday for Henpecked Husbands (1961)
- ❑ Holiday Time at Disneyland (1962)
- ❑ The Holland Story (1956)
- ❑ A Holster Full of Law (1961)
- ❑ The Horse of the West (1957)
- ❑ Horses for Greene (1961)
- ❑ How the West Was Lost (1967)
- ❑ How to Relax (1957)
- ❑ The Hunting Instinct (1961)
- ❑ Hurricane Hannah (1962)

I

- ❑ I Captured the King of the Leprechauns (1959)
- ❑ Ida, the Offbeat Eagle (1965)
- ❑ Inky the Crow (1969)
- ❑ In Shape with Von Drake (1964)
- ❑ Inside Donald Duck (1961)
- ❑ Inside Outer Space (1963)

J

- ❑   Joker, the Amiable Ocelot (1966)
- ❑   Journey to the Valley of the Emu (1978)
- ❑   Just Perfect (1990) MMC

K

- ❑   Kids is Kids (1961)
- ❑   Killers from Kansas (1959)
- ❑   Killers of the High Country (1959)
- ❑   Kentucky Gunslick (1960)
- ❑   Kraft Salutes Disneyland's 25, Anniversary (1980)

L

- ❑   The Last Electric Knight (1986)
- ❑   Law and Order, Incorporated (1958)
- ❑   Lawman or Gunman (1958)
- ❑   Lefty (1980)
- ❑   The Legend of El Blanco (1966)
- ❑   The Legend of Two Gypsy Dogs (1964)
- ❑   The Liberty Story (1957)
- ❑   Little Dog Lost (1963)
- ❑   The Little Shepherd Dog of Catalina (1973)

M

- ❑   The Mad Hermit of Chimney Butte (1960)

The Magical World of Disney (1988)

- ❑   Magic and Music (1958)
- ❑   Magic Highway, U.S.A. (1958)
- ❑   Major Effects (1979)
- ❑   Man and the Moon (1955)
- ❑   The Man from Bitter Creek (1959)
- ❑   Man in Flight (1957)
- ❑   Man in Space (1955)
- ❑   Man is His Own Worst Enemy (1962)
- ❑   Man on Wheels (1967)
- ❑   Mars and Beyond (1957)
- ❑   Mediterranean Cruise (1964)
- ❑   The Mickey Mouse Anniversary Show (1968)
- ❑   Mickey's 50 (1978)
- ❑   Mickey's Happy Valentine Special (1989)
- ❑   Mickey's 60th Birthday (1988)

- ❑ Minado, the Wolverine (1965)
- ❑ Mr. Boogedy (1986)
- ❑ Monsters of the Deep (1955)
- ❑ More About the Silly Symphonies (1957)
- ❑ Mountain Born (1972)
- ❑ The Mouseketeer Reunion (1980)
- ❑ The Mouseketeers at Walt Disney World (1977)
- ❑ Move Along, Mustang (1959)
- ❑ The Muppets at Walt Disney World (1990)
- ❑ Music for Everybody (1966)
- ❑ Mustang Man, Mustang Maid (1959)
- ❑ My Family is a Menagerie (1968)
- ❑ My Life as a Babysitter (1990) MMC
- ❑ The Mystery of Rustler's Cave (1977) MMC
- ❑ My Town (1986)

N

- ❑ The Nashville Coyote (1972)
- ❑ Nature's Better Built Homes (1969)
- ❑ Nature's Charter Tours (1968)
- ❑ Nature's Strangest Oddballs (1970)
- ❑ The New Adventures of Spin and Marty (1957-1958) MMC
- ❑ New True-Life Adventures (2000) x4
- ❑ The Nine Lives of Elfego Baca (1958)
- ❑ Nosey, the Sweetest Skunk in the World (1972)
- ❑ The Not So Lonely Lighthouse Keeper (1967)

O

- ❑ One Day at Teton Marsh (1964)
- ❑ One Day on Beetle Rock (1967)
- ❑ One Hour in Wonderland (1950)
- ❑ The 101 Problems of Hercules (1966)
- ❑ On Vacation (1956)
- ❑ Operation Undersea (1954)
- ❑ An Otter in the Family (1965)
- ❑ Our Friend the Atom (1957)
- ❑ Our Unsung Villains (1956)
- ❑ The Outlaw Cats of Colossal Cave (1975)
- ❑ The Owl That Didn't Give a Hoot (1968)

P

- ❑ Pacifically Peeking (1968)
- ❑ Pancho, the Fastest Paw in the West (1969)
- ❑ People and Places: Tiburon (1955)
- ❑ Perilous Assignment (1959)
- ❑ The Peter Tchaikovsky Story (1959)
- ❑ The Pigeon That Worked a Miracle (1958)
- ❑ The Plausible Impossible (1956)
- ❑ Pluto's Day (1956)
- ❑ The Postponed Wedding (1961)
- ❑ Prairie (1954)
- ❑ A Progress Report (1955)
- ❑ The Promised Land (1961)
- ❑ The Proud Bird from Shanghai (1973)

R

- ❑ Race for Survival (1978)
- ❑ A Rag, a Bone, a Box of Junk (1964)
- ❑ The Ranger of Brownstone (1968)
- ❑ A Ranger's Guide to Nature (1966)
- ❑ Range War at Tombstone (1959)
- ❑ Rapids Ahead (1960)
- ❑ Redcoat Strategy (1960)
- ❑ The Restless Sea (1964)
- ❑ Ringo, the Refugee Raccoon (1974)
- ❑ The Robber Stallion (1959)
- ❑ Runaway on the Rogue River (1974)
- ❑ Run, Light Buck, Run (1966)
- ❑ Rusty and the Falcon (1958)

S

- ❑ The Saga of Andy Burnett: Andy's First Chore (1957)
- ❑ The Saga of Andy Burnett: Andy's Initiation (1957)
- ❑ The Saga of Andy Burnett: Andy's Love Affair (1957)
- ❑ The Saga of Andy Burnett: The Big Council (1958)
- ❑ The Saga of Andy Burnett: The Land of Enemies (1958)
- ❑ The Saga of Andy Burnett: White Man's Medicine (1958)
- ❑ Salty, the Hijacked Harbor Seal (1972)
- ❑ A Salute to Alaska (1967)
- ❑ A Salute to Father (1961)
- ❑ San Juan River Expedition (1955-1956) MMC
- ❑ Searching for Nature's Mysteries (1956)

- ❑ Secret Bodyguard (1991) MMC
- ❑ The Secret of Lost Creek (1989) MMC
- ❑ The Secret of Mystery Lake (1956-1957) MMC
- ❑ The Secret of Old Glory Mine (1976)
- ❑ Seems There Was This Moose (1975)
- ❑ Shokee, the Everglades Panther (1974)
- ❑ Showdown at Sandoval (1959)
- ❑ The Silver Fox and Sam Davenport (1962)
- ❑ The Slaughter Trail (1959)
- ❑ Small & Frye (1983) x6
- ❑ Solomon, the Sea Turtle (1969)
- ❑ Spy in the Sky (1962)
- ❑ Square Peg in a Round Hole (1963)
- ❑ Star Tours (1986)
- ❑ A Storm Called Maria (1959)
- ❑ A Story of Dogs (1954)
- ❑ The Story of the Animated Drawing (1955)
- ❑ The Story of the Silly Symphony (1955)
- ❑ Superstar Goofy (1976)
- ❑ Survival in Nature (1956)
- ❑ The Survival of Sam the Pelican (1976)

T

- ❑ Tales of the Apple Dumpling Gang (1982)
- ❑ Teen Angel (1989) MMC
- ❑ Teen Angel Returns (1989) MMC
- ❑ Texas John Slaughter (1958)
- ❑ This is Your Life, Donald Duck (1960)
- ❑ Three on the Run (1978)
- ❑ Three Tall Tales (1963)
- ❑ The Titlemakers (1961)
- ❑ Toot, Whistle, Plunk and Boom (1959)
- ❑ Tory Vengeance (1960)
- ❑ To the South Pole for Science (1957)
- ❑ A Tribute to Joel Chandler Harris (1956)
- ❑ Tricks of Our Trade (1957)
- ❑ A Trip Thru Adventureland (1956)
- ❑ Trip to Tucson (1961)
- ❑ The Truth About Mother Goose (1963)
- ❑ Twister, Bull from the Sky (1976)
- ❑ Two Against the Arctic (1974)
- ❑ 2½ Dads (1986)
- ❑ Two Happy Amigos (1960)

V

- ❏ Varda, the Peregrine Falcon (1969)
- ❏ Von Drake in Spain (1962)

W

- ❏ The Wahoo Bobcat (1963)
- ❏ The Walt Disney Christmas Show (1951)
- ❏ Walt Disney: One Man's Dream (1981)
- ❏ Walt Disney World's 15, Birthday Celebration (1986)
- ❏ The Warrior's Path (1960)
- ❏ Welcome to the "World" (1975)
- ❏ The Whale's Tooth (1983)
- ❏ What I Want to Be (1955-1956) MMC
- ❏ Where Do the Stories Come From? (1956)
- ❏ Wild Burro of the West (1960)
- ❏ Wild Geese Calling (1969)
- ❏ Wild Heart (1968)
- ❏ Wild Horse Revenge (1959)
- ❏ The Wilderness Road (1961)
- ❏ Wild Jack (1989) x3
- ❏ Wildside (1985) x6
- ❏ A Woman's Courage (1961)
- ❏ Wonders of the Water World (1961)

Y

- ❏ The Yellowstone Story (1957)
- ❏ Your Host, Donald Duck (1957)

Z

- ❏ Zorro and Son (1983) x5

Appendix: Volume 1 Errata

While compiling *Disney Connections & Collections: Volume 2* I discovered that a small number of movies had somehow been missed out of Volume 1! Should Volume 1 receive an updated re-release, these missing movies will be included. In the meantime, here is the missing information for these Movies:

Monkeys, Go Home! (1967)

L'AUGHTER, L'AMOUR AND LE MONKEY BUSINESS! Madelaine, Monique, Delphine, Celeste... OO-LA-LA!

Source:
The Monkeys (1962) G.K. Wilkinson

Writers:
Maurice Tombragel

Director:
Andrew V. McLaglen

Stars:
Maurice Chevalier, Yvette Mimieux, Dean Jones

Premiere:
Feb 8, 1967

Length:
101 min

CONNECTIONS

Comic Strips:
Monkeys, Go Home! (TCT, Dec 4, 1966—Jan 29, 1967)

COLLECTIONS

Video/DVD:
2002

Blu-ray:
2016 Disney Movie Club Exclusive

Digital:
Amazon, iTunes, Vudu

Soundtrack:
1967 (LP)

Teacher's Pet (2004)

Be careful what you wish for. A musical tale about one dog's dream of becoming a boy.

Source:
Spin-off of *Teacher's Pet* (TV 2000-2002)

Writers:
Bill Steinkellner, Cheri Steinkellner

Director:
Timothy Björklund

Premiere:
Jan 16, 2004

Length:
73 min

COLLECTIONS

DVD:
2004

Digital:
Amazon, iTunes

Soundtrack:
2004 (CD)

Disney Princess Enchanted Tales: Follow Your Dreams (2007)

Source:
Sequel to *Sleeping Beauty* (1959) and *Aladdin and the King of Thieves* (DTV 1996)

Writers:
Shirley Pierce

Director:
David Block

Premiere:
Sep 4, 2007, DVD

Length:
56 min

COLLECTIONS
DVD/Blu-ray:
2007

Pooh's Super Sleuth Christmas Movie (2007)
AKA:
My Friends Tigger & Pooh: Super Sleuth Christmas Movie
Source:
Spin-off of *My Friends Tigger & Pooh* (2007-2010) TV series
Writers:
Nicole Dubuc, Brian Hohlfeld (story/screenplay), Jeff Kline (story)
Director:
Don MacKinnon
Premiere:
Nov 12, 2007, DVD (UK)
US Release:
Nov 20, 2007, DVD
Length:
44 min

CONNECTIONS
Movies:
- *Tigger & Pooh and a Musical Too* (DTV, 2009)
- *Super Duper Super Sleuths* (DTV, 2010)

COLLECTIONS
DVD:
2007

Tigger & Pooh and a Musical Too (2009)
Source:
Spin-off of *My Friends Tigger & Pooh* (2007-2010) TV series
Writers:
Nicole Dubuc, Dean Stefan (screenplay), Brian Hohlfled (story/screenplay)
Director:
David Hartman

Premiere:
Apr 7, 2009, DVD

Length:
58 min

COLLECTIONS

DVD:
2009

Soundtracks:
2009 (Digital)

Super Duper Super Sleuths (2010)

Source:
Spin-off of *My Friends Tigger & Pooh* (2007-2010) TV series

Writers:
Kim Beyer-Johnson

Director:
David Hartman

Premiere:
Apr 6, 2010, DVD

Length:
45 min

COLLECTIONS

DVD:
2010

You are welcome to report any omissions that you spot in *Disney Connections & Collections* to the author at jamesdoesdisney@outlook.com.

Further Reading

In researching this series, I have consulted and cross-checked many different websites and books to try and source the most accurate information. Below is a list of useful websites to help you find out more about some of the media mentioned in this Book:

- **Blu-ray.com**. Information relating to DVD and Blu-ray releases in the US and beyond. With reviews, cover artwork and region details.

- **Comic Vine** *comicvine.gamespot.com* and **Grand Comics Database** *comics.org*. Stories, cover images, biographical information and more.

- **D23: The Official Disney Fan Club** *d23.com*. The website of D23 includes an online, searchable version of Dave Smith's essential *Disney A-Z: The Official Encyclopedia*.

- **The Disney Wiki** *disney.wikia.com*. A Wiki dedicated to many, many aspects of the world of Disney, similar to Wikipedia.

- **DVDizzy.com**. An excellent DVD/Blu-ray review site, with dedicated Disney listings, featuring detailed reviews of movie releases and their content.

- **Giant Bomb** *giantbomb.com*. A curiously named database of computer games.

- **Internet Movie Database** *imdb.com*. For a whole host of information about individual movies. More accurate than Wikipedia, although not infallible.

- **JustWatch.com**. Find out where you can legally stream movies and TV shows in the US and beyond.

- **Soundtrack Collector** *soundtrackcollector.com*. Track listings and alternative versions of soundtracks on CD, LP and more.

- **The Ultimate Disney Books Network** *didierghez.com*. Updated regularly by Disney author Didier Ghez, this is the place to find out about Disney books already published and those yet to come, including those from Theme Park Press.

In addition, the following volumes are valuable sources of information about Disney TV movies and anthology shows (and comics):

- *Disney A-Z: The Official Encyclopedia* (5th Edition, 2016) Dave Smith.

- *The Wonderful World of Disney Television* (1997) Bill Cotter. Although lacking an index for easy reference, Cotter's volume covers a whole host of information about Disney television series, movies, specials and anthology shows.

- *Disney Comics: The Whole Story* (2016) Alberto Becattini. An essential guide to the whole world of Disney comics.

- *Sunday Nights with Walt: Everything I Know I Learned from "The Wonderful World of Disney"* (2017) Richard Rothrock. A personalised history of the Disney anthology TV show.

Acknowledgments

The Disney Connections & Collections series grew out of my PhD research, so I would once more like to thank my supervisors, Simon Popple and Dr Ian Macdonald who helped me through that process. I would also like to thank everyone who contributed to my audience research—that's over 3,500 people!

Theme Park Press' Bob McLain was one of the people generous enough to contribute to my research, and he later enthusiastically backed my proposal for these reference volumes. Thank you for fulfilling my dream of becoming a Disney author!

Thank you to all my friends who went out and bought (well, ordered online) a copy of my first book—and to everyone else who purchased volume 1. Particular thanks go to Ross and Matt, who I'm pretty certain bought the first copy—the first physical copy I got to hold!

As ever, my husband Andrew has supported me throughout—I couldn't have done it without him.

About the Author

Dr James R. Mason has enjoyed watching and collecting Disney movies since his parents bought him Disney Classics on VHS as a child. His personal interest eventually led to an academic interest. While studying for a Masters degree in Film Studies at the University of Bradford he kept returning to Disney for his papers and presentations, eventually writing a dissertation about the overlooked package features of the 1940s. From this came the inspiration for further study at the University of Leeds and the authoring of a PhD about Disney movies and their adult audiences.

James' PhD research gathered data on 390 Disney movies released to cinemas in the US between 1937 and 2015. He used this data to define a Disney film genre. At the same time he sought the opinions of adult audiences through an online questionnaire and focus groups that reached over 3,500 people. Then he compared audience perceptions of Disney movies with the movies themselves, revealing the biases that exist around animation and their implications for adult audiences and their appreciation of Disney movies.

Having earned his PhD in late 2017 through an examination that included animation scholar Professor Paul Wells, James works as a proofreader and copy editor. He continues to collect Disney media and longs to return to the Disney parks one day someday soon.

www.jamesdoes.co.uk

About Theme Park Press

Theme Park Press publishes books primarily about the Disney company, its history, culture, films, animation, and theme parks, as well as theme parks in general.

Our authors include noted historians, animators, Imagineers, and experts in the theme park industry.

We also publish many books by first-time authors, with topics ranging from fiction to theme park guides.

And we're always looking for new talent. If you'd like to write for us, or if you're interested in the many other titles in our catalog, please visit:

www.ThemeParkPress.com

Theme Park Press Newsletter

Subscribe to our free email newsletter and enjoy:

- Free book downloads and giveaways
- Access to excerpts from our many books
- Announcements of forthcoming releases
- Exclusive additional content and chapters
- And more good stuff available nowhere else

To subscribe, visit www.ThemeParkPress.com, or send email to newsletter@themeparkpress.com.

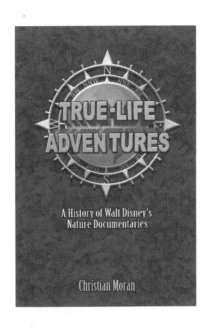

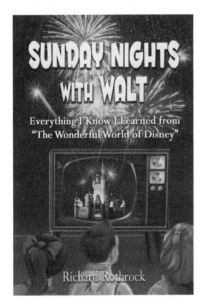

Read more about these books
and our many other titles at:

www.ThemeParkPress.com